The Gallaudet Dictionary of
American Sign Language

The Gallaudet Dictionary *of* American Sign Language

Clayton Valli, Editor in Chief

Illustrated by Peggy Swartzel Lott,
Daniel Renner, and Rob Hills

Gallaudet University Press • Washington, D.C.

Gallaudet University Press
Washington, DC 20002
gupress.gallaudet.edu

Paperback ISBN 978-1-954622-01-2
Ebook ISBN 978-1-954622-02-9

Library of Congress Cataloging in Publication Data
The Gallaudet dictionary of American Sign Language / Clayton Valli, editor
in chief ; illustrated by Peggy Swartzel Lott, Daniel Renner, and Rob Hills.
          p. cm.
ISBN 1-56368-282-6
1. American Sign Language—Dictionaries. 2. American Sign Language.
I. Valli, Clayton. II. Gallaudet University.
HV2475.G35 2005
419'.03—dc22

                                        2005051129

Thanks to the following people for serving as the sign models:

Lucinda Batch
Melissa S. Draganac-Hawk
Bonnie B. Gough
Monique B. Holt
Vadja V. Kolombatovic Jr.
Tayler Mayer
Erick Regan
David A. Rivera
Lauren Teruel

∞ The paper used in this publication meets the minimum requirements of the American
   National Standard for Information Sciences—Permanence of Paper for Printed Library
   Materials, ANSI Z39.48–1984

In memory of Clayton Valli—ASL linguist and poet. Clayton imbued every aspect of this dictionary with his knowledge and love of ASL.

Contents

Preface

The Gallaudet Dictionary of American Sign Language is a learning tool for beginning signers, a reference tool for more advanced signers, and also an English vocabulary reference for Deaf people. The signs are arranged in alphabetical order by the English word most commonly associated with each sign. This allows dictionary users to find the signs they need more easily. The rest of the English words associated with a given sign (in other words, the synonyms) are listed under the main entry, and all the words appear in the index.

The beginning position of each sign is drawn with a thin line and the final position is drawn with a heavy line. Arrows indicate the direction of the sign movements. All of the models in this dictionary are right-handed, and the signs are drawn from the receiver's perspective. Before copying a sign, right-handed signers should imagine themselves in the same position as the sign model. Left-handed signers should reverse the positions of the hands and the arrows and then mirror the signs on the page.

American Sign Language, like all languages, contains a lot of variation. This means that there are several ways to express the same concept. Often, the differences are a result of where a signer lives. The editors of this dictionary have included several versions of some signs, but their guiding principle was to choose the signs most commonly used in everyday conversation at Gallaudet University and in the Washington, D.C., area, which is a melting pot of ASL users from around the country. To achieve this goal, the dictionary contains more than 3,000 ASL signs.

Editorial Staff

Editor in Chief
Clayton Valli

Sign Master
Rosalyn F. Gannon

Senior Editors
Jean Gordon
Arlene Blumenthal Kelly

Editorial Contributor
Ceil Lucas

Project Manager
Jill K. Porco

Managing Editor
Ivey Pittle Wallace

Editorial Assistants
Stacey Bradford
Meredyth Mustafa-Julock

Introduction

A dictionary is a text that describes the meaning of words, often illustrates how they are used in context, and usually indicates how they are pronounced.

—Sidney Landau, *Dictionaries—The Art and Craft of Lexicography*

Sidney Landau's straightforward definition of dictionaries is a basic explanation of what dictionaries are, but they are much more than books of words and definitions. Landau recognized that "English dictionaries vary according to the variety of English they represent," and that they should clearly indicate either in their title or in their preface which variety they represent or which variety is primary.[1] Landau's observations are not new. In the first edition of his dictionary, Noah Webster stated that "it is not only important, but, in a degree necessary that the people of this country should have an *American Dictionary* of the English language" because there were real differences between British English and American English.[2] Both Webster and Landau recognized that a dictionary does not exist in a vacuum; rather, it is a reflection of the social community in which the language is used.

William C. Stokoe also recognized this reflection as he worked on the *Dictionary of American Sign Language* (DASL) with his deaf colleagues Dorothy Casterline and Carl Croneberg in the early 1960s.[3] Stokoe's inspiration for preparing the DASL came, in part, from the work of linguists George Trager and Henry Lee Smith, who "insisted that language could not be studied by itself, in isolation, but must be looked at in direct connection to the people who used it, the things they used it to talk about, and the view of the world that using it imposed on them."[4]

In this spirit, *The Gallaudet Dictionary of American Sign Language* provides a brief history of the American Deaf community and the creation of American Sign Language (ASL), as well as an explanation of its structure.

The American Deaf Community

ASL is the language used by members of the American Deaf community.* Estimates of the number of ASL users range from 500,000 to 2 million in the United States, and ASL is widely used in Canada as well.[5] The term "ASL users" includes many different kinds of people:

- Deaf members of a Deaf family whose primary language is ASL;
- hearing members of that same Deaf family who acquire ASL as a first language (such individuals are called "codas," that is, children of deaf adults);
- deaf members of hearing families who acquire ASL from their Deaf peers in residential school settings;
- late-deafened individuals who learn ASL as adults; and
- hearing people whose native language is English and who learn ASL as a second language.

Not much is known about the deaf people who lived in North America before 1817, but some came from Great Britain and Europe, and some were born here. Certain families in New England, notably on Martha's Vineyard and in New Hampshire and Maine, had several generations of deaf members. Deafness was so prevalent on Martha's Vineyard that many hearing Islanders knew and used the sign language of the deaf Islanders.[6] Because there was little direct contact between communities in the early nineteenth century, several kinds of sign language were probably used in America before 1817. In addition, hearing families that had a deaf child often developed *home signs*. These home signs included everything from pointing and miming to "a repertoire of agreed-upon gestures that convey a much more extensive range of information, sometimes even affective information."[7]

The year 1817 is significant in the history of ASL, as it is when the first permanent school for deaf children opened in the United States. In 1815, Thomas Hopkins Gallaudet, a Protestant minister from Hartford, Connecticut, traveled to Europe in search of a method for educating Alice Cogswell, the

*In this dictionary, an uppercase *D* denotes the community of language users who are culturally Deaf (i.e., share values, beliefs, and behaviors about deafness). A lowercase *d* refers to the deaf population in general and audiological deafness (i.e., the physiological condition of not being able to hear) in particular. Individuals who are deaf may not necessarily be Deaf.

deaf daughter of his neighbor, Dr. Mason Cogswell. Gallaudet went first to Great Britain to learn about the oral (speech only) method used in the Braidwood Schools in Scotland and near London. The directors of these schools had so many conditions for revealing their methods that Gallaudet declined to stay and observe their program. While in London, Gallaudet met Abbé Roch Ambroise Sicard, the director of the Royal Institution for the Deaf in Paris. Sicard was in London with Jean Massieu and Laurent Clerc, two former students who were then teachers in the institution. They were in London to demonstrate the school's manual (signing) teaching methods. Abbé Charles Michel de l'Epée, the founder and first director of the school in Paris, developed the method, which he called methodical signs. His system involved the use of French Sign Language in combination with a set of signs invented to represent parts of written and spoken French not found in French Sign Language. Sicard invited Gallaudet to the Royal Institution to learn French Sign Language and the school's teaching methods, and Gallaudet accepted his invitation.

When Gallaudet returned to the United States in the summer of 1816, Laurent Clerc came with him. On the ocean crossing, Clerc taught French Sign Language to Gallaudet and Gallaudet taught English to Clerc. Together, with Cogswell, they established the Connecticut Asylum for the Education and Instruction of Deaf and Dumb Persons—now called the American School for the Deaf—in April 1817.[8] Young deaf people from all parts of New England came to the school. Some of the deaf students, including those from Martha's Vineyard, brought their own sign language with them. They then learned the sign language used at the school, which, because of Clerc, included many French signs.[9]

It seems, then, that several language systems came in contact at the inception of the American School, giving rise to a new language that became a native language to the next generation of deaf teachers and pupils, especially those whose parents had attended the school. Furthermore, many of the graduates left New England and founded schools for the deaf in other parts of the country, and all these schools used the new language. By the time Clerc died in 1869, more than 1,500 pupils had graduated from the American School. In all, there were 30 residential schools across the United States providing an education to 3,246 deaf pupils, and 42 percent of the 187 teachers in these schools were deaf. Most of the deaf pupils and teachers married other deaf persons and roughly 10 percent had deaf children, which led to the further spread of ASL.[10] As languages are passed down to succeeding generations, they typically expand and change, so the language that developed at the American School during its early years and then spread across the United States was no doubt quite different from modern ASL.

The oral method for teaching deaf children, which predominated in England and Germany, did not emerge in the United States until the mid-nineteenth century. This method relied on speech and lipreading to the exclusion of sign language. Oral programs proliferated and dominated deaf education well into the twentieth century. Despite the controversies over the best way to communicate with and teach deaf children, ASL certainly did not disappear from the lives of Deaf people; they continued to sign in their homes and in social interactions with other Deaf people. Deaf children in the residential schools were routinely punished for using ASL in their classrooms, but they never stopped signing in the dormitories. Since most deaf children (90 percent) are born into hearing families and have no automatic access to ASL, deaf children from Deaf families played a crucial role in teaching the language to their peers and socializing them into the Deaf world.[11] To this day, residential schools have very special status in the Deaf community as the sites where Deaf culture is transmitted to deaf children. In fact, recent demographic research indicates that many deaf students who have deaf parents attend residential schools for the deaf, while the vast majority of deaf children who have hearing parents are mainstreamed into programs with hearing children.[12]

Formal and widespread acceptance of ASL as a language did not begin until the 1960s, when Stokoe wrote a description of its linguistic structure and then published the *Dictionary of American Sign Language* with Casterline and Croneberg.[13] At the time, Stokoe was an English professor at Gallaudet University, the world's only liberal arts university for deaf students. He began his research after noticing that his students' sign language had a distinctly different grammar from English. After reading Stokoe's work, both hearing and deaf people began to recognize ASL as a language in its own right. Prior to this time, most hearing people thought ASL was simply a collection of gestures, a form of mime, or a kind of broken English. Fluent signers did not have a name for their language—they referred to it simply as "sign" or "the sign language." Stokoe's groundbreaking work established the legitimacy of

ASL as a language, and, as a result, attitudes toward sign language changed among Deaf people as well as among some of the hearing people who worked with them.

In the early 1970s, many residential schools and public school deaf education programs began to use sign language again. They adopted the philosophy of Total Communication, which encouraged teachers to use any means available—signing, fingerspelling, talking, and speechreading (lipreading)—to communicate with deaf children. Many teachers began to sign and talk at the same time to their deaf students.[14] This practice, which came to be known as Sign-Supported Speech, has produced mixed results in deaf students' fluency in ASL as well as in English.[15] Today, many different communication systems can be found in classrooms around the country. Some teachers use ASL only, some use a bilingual (ASL–English) approach, others use Sign-Supported Speech, and still others use the oral approach.

ASL as a Language

ASL is a visual-manual language with a structure independent of and very different from spoken English. Users of ASL do not speak English while they sign, and the sign order of ASL is sometimes very different from the word order of spoken English. Signers also can convey grammatical information with their faces, bodies, and the surrounding space.

Like all languages, ASL is productive—an infinite number of sentences can be produced from a finite set of rules, and new messages can be created at any time. ASL can be used to discuss any topic, from the concrete to the abstract, from basic survival to philosophy and physics. It can be used to discuss the past, the future, and nonimmediate situations; it is not restricted to the present and the immediate. ASL is used as the medium of instruction in classrooms from the preschool level through college and graduate school, and for all subjects ranging from math and chemistry to literature and linguistics. In addition, ASL is used for creative purposes such as storytelling, word games, and poetry, which has led to a reconsideration of the meaning of literature. A body of ASL literature clearly exists in the form of videotaped poems and stories.[16]

ASL is composed of symbols that are organized and used systematically. These symbols are manual signs produced with the hands and nonmanual signs produced with the face, head, and body. Like words, signs represent concepts. For writing purposes, we use small capital letters to represent the meaning of signs. These representations are called *glosses,* and they help to distinguish signs from English words and acronyms, like ASL. Many sign glosses correspond to one English word, but because signs represent concepts, they sometimes can correspond to an English phrase. When a sign is glossed as two or more English words, the glosses are connected by hyphens. For example, where English requires two words for the concepts "stand up" and "lie down," ASL uses one sign for each concept, but the glosses are written as STAND-UP and LIE-DOWN. One ASL sign may also correspond to several English words that have similar meaning. For example, the ASL sign PRETTY is used to express the English words *pretty, beautiful,* and *lovely.* Similarly, some English concepts that are conveyed in one word require more than one sign. The word *Bible* is signed as GOD⌒BOOK or JESUS⌒BOOK, and *sister* is signed as GIRL⌒SAME.

Unlike most English idioms, which are full sentences or phrases (such as "miss the boat" and "kick the bucket"), some ASL idioms consist of one sign and, therefore, are included in this dictionary. Examples include TRAIN-GONE, which means "you missed your chance;" SAME-SAME, which means "it's the same old thing;" and the sign WHAT'S-UP. Classifier predicates, which will be explained in a separate section, also are single signs that correspond to an entire English phrase, and so they are included in the dictionary.

The Structure of Signs

Manual signs have five parameters, or parts: the **handshape**, which is the specific configuration of the hand(s); the **location** of the hand(s)—on the body, on the head, in the space in front of the body; the **movement** of the hand(s)—up and down, side to side, in an arc; the **orientation** of the palm(s)—up or down, facing the signer or facing away from the signer; and **nonmanual signals**, which include obligatory facial expressions, eye gaze, specific head positions, or particular body positions. Each sign includes all these parameters, so changing even one parameter may create a new sign. For example, the signs SUMMER, UGLY, and DRY share the same handshape, palm orientation, and movement, but they differ in location and, thus, in meaning.

SUMMER   UGLY   DRY

Handshape. Many of the handshapes used in ASL signs come from the American manual alphabet and numbers. These handshapes represent the 26 letters of the English alphabet (see next page) and the numbers 1–10. The handshapes used with signs are often arbitrary, but sometimes they carry specific meaning. For the sign PREACH, the tip of the index finger touches the tip of the thumb, and the middle, ring, and pinky fingers are extended. This handshape is arbitrary; it does not add any information to the sign. However, this particular handshape is also the sign for the number 9, and when it is used to make the signs WEEK, MONTH, and other time designations, it creates the meaning of 9 weeks, 9 months, and so forth.

Movement. Signs, like spoken words, have a specific structure. Spoken-language words consist of a sequence of consonants and vowels, and signs consist of a sequence of holds and movements. During a hold, the hand is stationary and does not change in any way; a movement occurs when some part of the sign—the handshape, the palm orientation, the location, the facial expression—is in the process of changing.[17]

The way the hands move is central to the structure and meaning of signs. In one class of signs, the repetition of the movement marks the difference between a verb and its related noun. If the sign consists of just one movement, then the sign is a verb; if the movement is repeated, then the sign is a noun. Examples of noun-verb pairs include CHAIR/SIT, AIRPLANE/FLY, and NEWSPAPER/PRINT.[18] In another class of signs, the movement is repeated to show that a noun is plural rather than singular.

The American Manual Alphabet

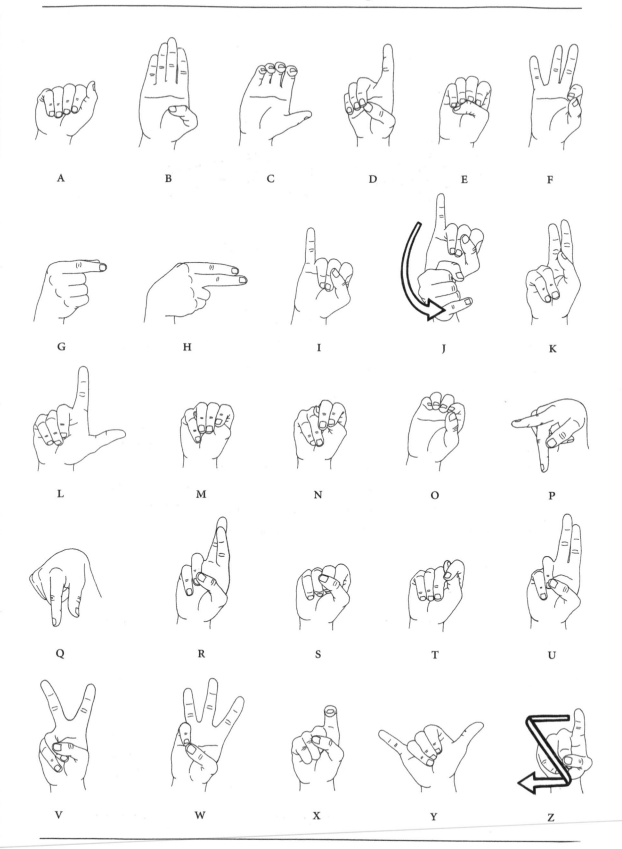

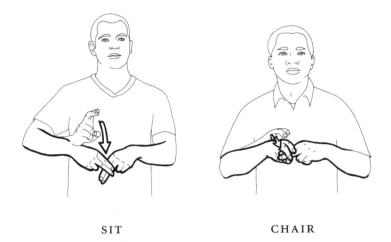

SIT   CHAIR

Movement is also important for distinguishing among signs that have related meaning. For example, the concepts *big, huge,* and *enormous* are very similar, and so are the signs for these concepts. The handshape, palm orientation, and location of the signs are the same, but the size of the movement creates the change in meaning.

Nonmanual Signals. Most signs in everyday conversation are made with a neutral facial expression. However, there are signs that require a particular facial expression or nonmanual signal to make the meaning clear. The illustrations in this dictionary include appropriate facial expressions. The signs PAH ("finally"), RECENTLY, and NOT-YET are good examples of how facial expression and nonmanual signals are incorporated into a sign.

PAH   RECENTLY   NOT-YET

The same sequence of words or signs in a sentence can have a variety of meanings, depending on the accompanying nonmanual signals and the social context in which the sentence occurs. For example, the simple declarative spoken sentence *They bought a house* can become a question by changing the emphasis on one or more words and by using a rising inflection in the voice—*They bought a **house**?* In ASL, the sequence of signs HOME YOU can be a declarative sentence *(You are home)*, a yes/no question *(Are you home?* or *Are you going home?)*, an imperative *(Go home!)*, or an indirect request *(Can I get a ride home with you?)*, depending on the context and the nonmanual signals used by the signer. For the yes/no question, the signer would raise her eyebrows and tilt her head forward, but for the imperative sentence, she would assume a stern expression.

Arbitrary and Iconic Signs

ASL signs may be arbitrary or iconic. Arbitrary signs do not reflect the form or movement of the object, activity, or concept they represent. Examples of arbitrary signs include WRONG and HOW. Nothing about the execution of these signs reveals their meaning. Iconic signs, however, do reveal information about their meaning. Some part of the sign depicts an aspect of the thing or event being represented. For example, the position of the arm and the handshape used in the sign TREE visually represent the trunk and branches of a tree. The location and movement of the sign CAT represent a cat's whiskers. The fact that many signs are iconic does not mean that ASL is basically mime or a collection of "pictures in the air." ASL has a complex linguistic structure, as do all signed languages.

WRONG

TREE

Expanding the Lexicon

Fingerspelling. All languages have the ability to add new concepts into their lexicon (vocabulary), and ASL is no exception. One of the newest signs in ASL is PAGER (see p. 321). ASL also adds new signs through the use of classifiers (see pp. xxvii–xl). New concepts are often introduced first by fingerspelling, that is, by using the manual alphabet to spell out each letter in an English word. These signs are produced individually in sequence to spell a word that does not have a sign equivalent. Deaf people often fingerspell proper nouns, especially names, and new concepts. They always fingerspell their names when introducing themselves—J-O-H-N, C-E-L-E-S-T-E, etc.—and they fingerspell new English words until a sign is created and accepted. Fingerspelling is a key component of ASL. In fact, it is much more widely used in ASL than in other sign languages.[19] Thus, this dictionary contains many examples of fingerspelled words, as well as a list of English words that are fingerspelled rather than signed (see p. xli).

Borrowing from Other Languages. Signed languages, like spoken languages, are not universal. American Sign Language is completely distinct from British Sign Language, Italian Sign Language, and every other country's sign language. Deaf people who know one sign language do not automatically understand another sign language, but they do learn other sign languages when they come in contact with them. The ease of international travel has made it much more common for Deaf people to meet at international conferences and sports competitions. As a result of this contact, ASL has begun to replace its signs for other countries with the signs used by the Deaf people in those countries (see ITALY, for example). This is another way to add new signs to the ASL lexicon.

(U.S. SIGN)

(ITALIAN SIGN)

ITALY

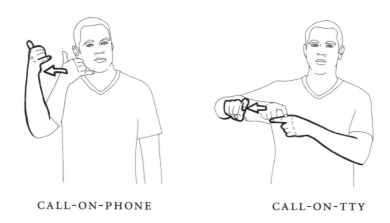

CALL-ON-PHONE   CALL-ON-TTY

Changes over Time. Like all other languages, ASL has changed over time. These changes occur in all parts of the language—handshapes change, locations change, the orientation of the palm changes, two-hand signs become one-hand, one-hand signs become two-hand, and whole signs change as a result of new technologies in society. For example, the old sign for TELEPHONE consisted of two S handshapes (a closed fist), one at the signer's ear and one at the mouth, an iconic sign reflecting early telephone technology. The current sign is a Y handshape (thumb and pinky extended, all other fingers bent into the palm) held at the signer's ear. Similarly, one of the signs for the phrase "make a call" is a variation of the current sign TELEPHONE, while the other sign means "make a call on a TTY," the teletypewriter used by Deaf people to communicate over phone lines. This sign is produced by moving the tip of the bent right index finger along the extended left index finger.

Variation

ASL is a language shared by a large national community of users, but smaller communities exist within the larger ASL community. These smaller communities use signs that differ in varying degrees from one another. This is called *variation,* and it occurs in spoken and signed languages across various regions of the country, as well as between members of smaller communities living in the same area. *Signs Across America,* a collection of regional differences in ASL, contains 1,200 signs for 130 English words. The authors found as many as 21 different signs meaning *birthday,* 22 signs meaning *picnic,* and 7 signs meaning *interesting,* among others. Other researchers have found that African American signers sign differently from white signers, older signers use different signs than do younger signers, deaf-blind signers sign differently from sighted signers, and deaf children of Deaf parents sign differently from deaf children of hearing parents.[20] Because certain variants are widely known and accepted, this dictionary contains two or more versions of some signs.

Contact Between Languages

The American Deaf community is fundamentally bilingual. In other words, most American signers comfortably use two languages—ASL and English. In situations like this, where the languages are in contact every day, each can influence the other in a number of ways. One of the most common occurrences is called *lexical borrowing,* that is, one language borrows words or signs from another language. An example from spoken English and French contact is the French term *le weekend.* An example from ASL is the adoption of the Italian Sign Language sign for "Italy."

There are several ways that English and ASL borrow from each other. The first is fingerspelling (see p. xxi), which allows signers to spell English words letter by letter. Some English words, like *job, back,* and *fax,* are so short that signers prefer to spell them. Very often the transition between the separate letter signs becomes so fluid that some of the signs are even omitted. This is called *lexicalization.* In these cases, fingerspelling becomes more like signing—instead of spelling J-O-B, for instance, a signer will make a J and a B in one smooth movement. The written versions of lexicalized signs are marked with the pound (#) symbol (for example, #JOB, and #BACK). *The Gallaudet Dictionary of American Sign Language* contains many examples of lexicalized signs as well as abbreviations that are preferred over signs for words like *air conditioning* (A-C) and *refrigerator* (R-E-F). The dictionary also includes a list of English words that usually are fingerspelled instead of signed (see p. xli).

ASL borrows English words to create compound signs—BOY⌢ FRIEND, HOME⌢WORK, and HOME⌢SICK are all borrowed from English. These compounds consist of two ASL signs that together express an English concept. ASL also has compounds that combine fingerspelling and signs. The ASL compound sign LIFE⌢#STYLE is made by first signing LIFE and then fingerspelling "style."[21]

#JOB   #BACK   A–C

Another result of language contact is *codeswitching*, or the use of a word or sign from one language while speaking/signing another language. Bilingual signers as well as bilingual speakers occasionally switch back and forth between two languages. In the case of English and ASL, hearing signers may stop speaking English and momentarily switch to ASL; Deaf signers may stop signing to mouth an English word or phrase. Signers sometimes sign in English word order for emphasis or to quote an English sentence exactly.

The final outcome of language contact between ASL and English is a kind of signing called Contact Signing. Its structure combines elements of both languages.[22] Contact Signing consists of ASL signs in English word order and frequently includes continuous mouthing (talking without voice). Isolated mouthing does occur in ASL; some of the mouthing is directly traceable to related English words, and some of it is completely unrelated to spoken English. However, this mouthing is quite different from the continuous mouthing that occurs in Contact Signing, and neither ASL nor Contact Signing allows for simultaneously speaking and signing. Contact Signing incorporates the ASL practice of using space, body shifting, pointing (indexing), and eye gaze to set up topics and subsequently refer to them throughout a conversation. It is not codified and it cannot be formally taught; rather, it occurs quite naturally as a result of contact among bilinguals.

Like spoken-language bilinguals, individuals who are bilingual in a signed language and a spoken/written language will borrow, codeswitch, and fingerspell for a very simple reason: because they can. That is, human beings in language contact situations exploit whatever linguistic resources are available to them; so, given the availability of two modalities, (a spoken language and a signed language) and competence in them, they will use both of them. In some ways, there is nothing exceptional about language contact in the Deaf community. There are two unique things about it, however. First, no one can predict how the two modalities will be used. Deaf people may mouth to other Deaf people and not use their hands at all; hearing bilinguals may sign to each other when no Deaf people are around; a Deaf person may speak to a hearing person and the hearing person may answer in ASL with no voice; a Deaf and a hearing person may produce contact signing with each other, and so forth. Second, because two modalities are involved, some unusual outcomes (such as fingerspelling) are possible. What remains predictable and clear is that ASL and other signed languages are viable and autonomous linguistic systems highly valued by the members of Deaf communities all over the world.

Notes

Much of the discussion in the introduction and the section on classifiers is adapted from Clayton Valli, Ceil Lucas, and Kristin J. Mulrooney, *Linguistics of American Sign Language,* 4th ed. (Washington, DC: Gallaudet University Press, 2005), and from Ceil Lucas and Clayton Valli, "American Sign Language," in *Language in the U.S.A: Themes for the 21st Century,* ed. Edward Finegan and John Rickford (Cambridge: Cambridge University Press, 2004).

1. Sidney Landau, *Dictionaries: The Art and Craft of Lexicography* (Cambridge: Cambridge University Press, 2001), 6, 12.

2. Noah Webster, *An American Dictionary of the English Language* (New York : S. Converse, 1828); quoted in Howard Webber, "Preface," *Webster's II New Riverside University Dictionary* (Itasca, IL: Riverside Publishing Company, 1998), 7.

3. William C. Stokoe, Dorothy Casterline, and Carl Croneberg, *A Dictionary of American Sign Language on Linguistic Principles* (Washington, DC: Gallaudet College Press, 1965).

4. William C. Stokoe, "A Sign Language Dictionary," in *The Deaf Way,* ed. Carol J. Erting, Robert C. Johnson, Dorothy L. Smith, and Bruce D. Snider (Washington, DC: Gallaudet University Press, 1994), 333.

5. Jerome D. Schein, *At Home Among Strangers* (Washington, DC: Gallaudet University Press, 1989).

6. Harlan Lane, Richard C. Pillard, and Mary French, "Origins of the American Deaf-World: Assimilating and Differentiating Societies and Their Relation to Genetic Patterning," *Sign Language Studies* 1 (2000): 17–44; Nora Groce, *Everyone Here Spoke Sign Language* (Cambridge, MA: Harvard University Press, 1985).

7. Harlan Lane, Robert Hoffmeister, and Ben Bahan, *A Journey into the DEAF-WORLD* (San Diego: Dawn Sign Press, 1996), 39–40.

8. John Vickrey Van Cleve and Barry Crouch, *A Place of Their Own: Creating the Deaf Community in America* (Washington, DC: Gallaudet University Press, 1989), 32–45.

9. James Woodward, "Historical Bases of American Sign Language," in *Understanding Language through Sign Language Research,* ed. Patricia Siple (New York: Academic Press, 1978), 333–348. Woodward compared 87 modern French Sign Language (LSF) and ASL signs and found that 58 percent of the signs were the same or very similar for the same concept. This represents a high degree of overlap between the two languages.

10. Lane, Hoffmeister, and Bahan, *Journey into the DEAF-WORLD,* 57, 58.

11. Van Cleve and Crouch, *A Place of Their Own,* 151.

12. Claire Ramsey, *Deaf Children in Public Schools—Placement, Context, and Consequences,* Sociolinguistics in Deaf Communities, vol. 3 (Washington, DC: Gallaudet University Press, 1997), 34.

13. William C. Stokoe, *Sign Language Structure: An Outline of the Visual Communication Systems of the American Deaf,* Studies in Linguistics, 8 (Buffalo: University of Buffalo, 1960); Stokoe, Croneberg, and Casterline, *Dictionary of American Sign Language.*

14. David M. Denton, *The Philosophy of Total Communication,* Supplement to the *British Deaf News* (Carlisle: The British Deaf Association, 1976).

15. Robert E. Johnson, Scott K. Liddell, and Carol J. Erting, "Unlocking the Curriculum: Principles for Achieving Access in Deaf Education" (Gallaudet Research Institute Working Paper 89-3, Gallaudet University, Washington, DC, 1989).

16. Clayton Valli, "Poetics of American Sign Language" (Ph.D. diss., Union Institute, 1993).

17. Scott Liddell and Robert E. Johnson, "ASL: The Phonological Base," *Sign Language Studies* 64 (1989): 195–277.

18. Ted Supalla and Elissa Newport, "How Many Seats in a Chair? The Derivation of Nouns and Verbs in American Sign Language," in *Understanding Language through Sign Language Research,* ed. Patricia Siple (New York: Academic Press, 1978), 91–132.

19. Carol Padden, "Learning Fingerspelling Twice: Young Signing Children's Acquisition of Fingerspelling," in *Advances in the Sign Language Development of Deaf Children,* ed. Brenda Schick, Marc Marschark, and Patricia E. Spencer (New York: Oxford University Press, forthcoming).

20. Edgar H. Shroyer and Susan P. Shroyer, *Signs Across America: A Look at Regional Differences in American Sign Language* (Washington, DC: Gallaudet University Press, 1984); Anthony Aramburo, "Sociolinguistics of the Black Deaf Community," in *The Sociolinguistics of the Deaf Community,* ed. Ceil Lucas (San Diego: Academic Press, 1989), 103–19; John Lewis, "Ebonics in American Sign Language: Stylistic Variation in African American Signers," in *Deaf Studies V: Toward 2000—Unity and Diversity* (Washington, DC: College for Continuing Education, Gallaudet University, 1998); Ceil Lucas, Robert Bayley, and Clayton Valli, *Sociolinguistic Variation in ASL,* Sociolinguistics in Deaf Communities, vol. 7 (Washington, DC: Gallaudet University Press, 2001).

21. Arlene B. Kelly, "Fingerspelling Use Among the Deaf Senior Citizens of Baltimore," in *School of Communication Student Forum,* ed. Elizabeth A. Winston (Washington, DC: Gallaudet University School of Communication,1991), 90–98.

22. Ceil Lucas and Clayton Valli, *Language Contact in the American Deaf Community* (San Diego: Academic Press, 1992).

Classifiers in American Sign Language

Classifiers are an important component of ASL. They allow signers to express whole phrases with a single sign. Unlike English, which has very few classifiers, ASL has many and they are used quite often. Classifiers are a critical element of ASL sentence structure.

Sentences in all languages consist of two basic parts—a *subject* and a *predicate*. The subject contains the person, thing, idea, or activity described in the sentence, and the words or signs used in the subject are called nouns or noun phrases. The predicate contains the words or signs that describe the action performed by the subject or that say something about the subject. Predicates are not limited to verbs or action words, as the following English sentences illustrate.

Sentence	Subject	Predicate
The dog ran down the street.	*The dog*	*ran down the street*
The twins play soccer.	*The twins*	*play soccer*
David is home.	*David*	*is home*
Lynne feels sick.	*Lynne*	*feels sick*

Some languages, including ASL, do not use the verb *to be* (*is/are, was/were, will*). In these languages, a predicate can be a verb, a noun, or an adjective. Some ASL sentences contain only one sign in the subject and one sign in the predicate. Examples include BABY SLEEP (*the baby is sleeping*), which is a noun and a verb; GIRL HOME (*the girl is home*), which is a noun and a noun; and CAT HUNGRY (*the cat is hungry*), which is a noun and an adjective. These last two examples do not include the verb *is*, but the noun

HOME and the adjective HUNGRY function as predicates; in other words, they say something about the nouns GIRL and CAT. Verbs, nouns, and adjectives can be predicates in ASL.

ASL has another group of predicates called *classifier predicates*. Classifier predicates are signs that represent a particular class, or type, of objects. These objects include, but are not limited to, people, animals, piles, poles, vehicles, and surfaces. Classifiers are made with specific handshapes, and they carry very specific meanings. An entire phrase can be expressed with one classifier predicate (in other words, one sign). For example, in the sentence *The boy rolled down the hill,* the signer will first sign BOY and then will use one sign to show exactly how the boy rolled down the hill.

All of the sign parameters discussed in the introduction—handshape, movement, location, orientation, and nonmanual signals—are used in classifier predicates, though the handshape and movement provide the primary meaning. The location information reveals the beginning and ending points of the action. The nonmanual signals relay descriptive information about the subject. For example, a signer will purse her lips when describing thin objects and will puff out her cheeks when describing fat or thick objects.

The handshapes used in classifier predicates are called *classifier handshapes*. Many of these handshapes are manual alphabet and number signs; others are modifications of these signs (see p. xviii for the American Manual Alphabet; some of the modified signs are shown in the chart on page xxix). Classifier handshapes convey a specific type of information, so they are not interchangeable. The handshape that represents a person cannot be used to describe a flat object, nor can the handshape used to represent a round cylinder be used to describe a vehicle.

Researchers have found that classifier predicates have three different kinds of movements, which are called *movement roots*. The three types of movement roots are *stative descriptive, contact,* and *process.** These movements, in combination with the classifier handshapes, produce classifier predicates. Not all of the classifier handshapes can be used with all three of

---

*Ted Supalla first identified movement roots and classifier handshapes in his dissertation, "Structure and Acquisition of Verbs of Motion and Location in American Sign Language" (University of California, San Diego, 1978). Scott Liddell and Robert E. Johnson further elaborated on them in "An Analysis of Spatial Locative Predicates in American Sign Language" (presentation, Fourth International Symposium on Sign Language Research, July 15–19, 1987)

Modified Handshapes

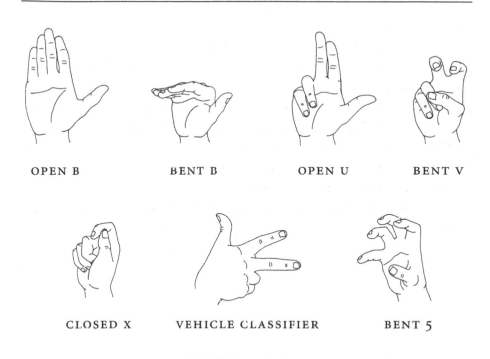

OPEN B   BENT B   OPEN U   BENT V

CLOSED X   VEHICLE CLASSIFIER   BENT 5

the movement roots. The following section explains each of the movement roots and the types of classifier handshapes associated with them.

Stative Descriptive Movement Roots

In this group of movement roots, the hand describes the state or condition of an object—in other words, the physical appearance or characteristics of the object. However, the movement of the hand does not mean that the object itself is moving. Rather, the movement is part of the description. Some of the classifier handshapes that occur with stative descriptive movement roots are listed below.

Surface Handshapes

These handshapes represent thin surfaces or wires, narrow surfaces, or wide surfaces. The handshapes in this group include the B handshape, which is used to represent a large flat area (like an expanse of desert), an uphill incline, or a bumpy surface.

Depth and Width Handshapes

The classifier handshapes in this group show the depth and width of different things, such as tree trunks and pipes. The F, C, and L handshapes are often used and each represents the thickness of the object being described. The 5 handshape is used to represent layers or depth, such as the amount of snow on the ground. The G and L handshapes are used to describe stripes of various widths.

Extent Handshapes

Handshapes in this group represent amounts or volumes, such as the amount of liquid in a glass (the G handshape) and the height of a stack of papers (the 5 handshape).

Perimeter-Shape Handshapes

These handshapes symbolize the external shape of an object. Rectangular and circular shapes are made with 1 handshapes. The L handshape is used for small rectangular objects, such as envelopes, note cards, and checks.

On-Surface Handshapes

The handshapes in this group represent large groups or crowds of people, animals, or objects. For example, the Bent 5 handshape is used to describe an audience or a herd of animals. The Bent 5 handshape also indicates a mound. The 4 handshape signifies many people standing in line.

Stative Descriptive Movement Roots:
Surface and Depth and Width Handshapes

LONG-FLAT-SURFACE

FLAT-SURFACE-
GOING-UPHILL

Surface Handshapes

THIN-POLE

WIDE-POLE

THIN-PIPE

WIDE-PIPE

THIN-STRIPES

WIDE-STRIPES

Depth and Width Handshapes

Stative Descriptive Movement Roots:
Extent, Perimeter-Shape, and On-Surface Handshapes

FLAT-PILE-THIS-HIGH   THIS-MUCH-LIQUID

Extent Handshapes

RECTANGULAR-   ROUND-OBJECT   SMALL-RECTANGULAR-
OBJECT   OBJECT

Perimeter-Shape Handshapes

AUDIENCE   PEOPLE-STANDING-   MOUND
                          IN-LINE

On-Surface Handshapes

Contact Movement Roots

A contact movement root establishes the location and orientation of an object, and it means *located in a specific place*. The hand moves downward to show the location, not to mean that the object is moving. The movement of the contact root creates such classifier predicates as SIT-DOWN and LOCATED-THERE. The following handshapes usually occur with a contact movement root.

Whole Entity Handshapes

The Bent V handshape is used in contact roots to represent a person sitting, and it can mean *sit on the chair,* or *sit around the table.* It also is used to symbolize animals sitting. To sign the ASL sentence CAT SIT, a signer will make the sign CAT and then change the hand to a Bent V handshape and move it straight down to create the classifier predicate ANIMAL-SIT. This same predicate can be used to say something about a bird, a dog, a squirrel, and other small animals. The upside-down V handshape signifies a person standing, while the 1 handshape means a person is located in a particular place. The F handshape is used to show the location of small round objects, such as coins, poker chips, and buttons.

Perimeter-Shape Handshapes

Perimeter-shape handshapes can occur with stative descriptive movement roots and with contact movement roots. Combined with a contact movement root, these handshapes show where an object is located. For example, L handshapes can represent a picture frame and the movement shows where the picture is placed on a wall.

On-Surface Handshapes

A Bent 5 handshape can be used with a contact root to mean CITY-BE-LOCATED. The hands move straight out from the signer, as if indicating points on an imaginary map, to sign sentences such as BALTIMORE THERE, D.C. HERE.

PERSON-SITTING

PERSON STANDING

COINS

BUTTONS-ON-A-SHIRT

Whole-Entity Handshapes

PICTURE-ON-THE-WALL
Perimeter-Shape Handshapes

Process Movement Roots

The action performed by the hand or hands in this group of movement roots corresponds to the actual movement of the object being described. Many different classifier handshapes are used with process movement roots.

Whole Entity Handshapes

Just as they do with stative descriptive movement roots, whole entity handshapes refer to an entire object, such as a car, an animal, a person, or a group of people. Whole entity handshapes also can represent airplanes, flying saucers, and paper. Suppose a signer is describing that he saw a car drive down the street. He would first sign CAR and then he would produce a 3 handshape turned on its side, with the palm facing in, and he would move his hand from one point to another. In this sentence, the 3 handshape represents the car. This classifier handshape is the symbol for the class of objects called VEHICLE, and it is used to show the movement of a car, a boat, or a bicycle. The movement, orientation, and location can change to show how the vehicle moved. The classifier predicate in the sentence just described is VEHICLE-DRIVE-BY, and its English equivalent is *A car drives by*.

The 1 handshape can be used to represent one person. If a signer was talking about a woman who walked by, he would use the same movement just described for the car, but he would use a 1 handshape. The 1 handshape signifies an individual person. The ASL sentence would be WOMAN PERSON-PASS-BY, or *A woman passes by* in English. If a signer meant to sign VEHICLE-DRIVE-BY but used a 1 handshape, the sentence would not make sense to those watching because this classifier handshape represents a person, not a car.

The V handshape characterizes specific movements that people make. For example, turning the hand upside down and moving it to the left while wiggling the index and middle fingers back and forth creates the classifier predicate meaning *person walk by*. Bringing the V hand up and over to land on the palm means *person get up,* and placing the back of the V hand on the opposite palm means *person lie down.*

VEHICLE-GO-BY

BOAT-SAILING-ALONG

PERSON-GO-BY

TWO-PEOPLE-WALKING-
TOWARD-EACH-OTHER

PERSON-WALK-BY

PERSON-STAND-UP

Instrumental Handshapes

The handshapes in this category symbolize hands holding different objects or instruments as they do something with these objects. They include the F handshape for picking up a piece of paper; the C handshape for peeling an orange; the C and F handshapes for picking up cups of various kinds (for example, a paper cup and a tea cup) and for holding thick and thin objects; the Bent 5 handshape for turning a door knob; the X handshape, with the thumb touching the tip of the index finger, for dealing playing cards; and other representative handshapes to show the action of using scissors, knives, tweezers, hair brushes, paint brushes, rakes, video cameras, syringes, baseball bats, golf clubs, and keys.

Processs Movement Roots: Instrumental Handshapes

PEEL-A-THIN-
SUBSTANCE

PEEL-A-THICK-
SUBSTANCE

TURN-A-KEY

TURN-A-DOORNOB

Process Movement Roots: Instrumental Handshapes (continued)

PAINT-ON-A-SMALL-SURFACE

PAINT-ON-A-LARGE-SURFACE

BRUSH-HAIR

DEAL-CARDS

Extent Handshapes

In addition to being used with stative descriptive movement roots, extent handshapes also show how much an object moves. The bent hand creates the classifier predicates TIRE-LOSING-AIR and FLAT-TIRE. Using both hands in C handshapes, a signer can show a balloon filling with air.

Surface Handshapes

With a process movement root, surface handshapes show how different kinds of surfaces move. The 4 handshape represents liquid dripping and is used in sentences such as *The water is running* and *My nose is running.* The B handshape can indicate a flat surface, such as a moving conveyer belt, or it can signify water flowing in a river or ocean.

Using Classifier Predicates

The location of every classifier predicate typically represents a location in three-dimensional space. If a signer produces the VEHICLE classifier with a contact movement root in a particular point in space, she means that a vehicle is located at that point in three-dimensional space. She will then move her hand to show exactly how far the vehicle traveled.

Different handshapes may be used to represent the same object or concept in a classifier predicate, depending on the context in a particular sentence. For example, a signer will use a B handshape to place a piece of paper

---

Processs Movement Roots: Extent and Surface Handshapes

| TIRE-LOSING-AIR | FLAT-TIRE | PILE-DECREASING |

Extent Handshapes

| RUNNING-WATER | RUNNY-NOSE | WATER-FLOWING |

Surface Handshapes

---

on a table and an F handshape to pick up that same piece of paper. These handshapes represent the shape and depth of the object. The G handshapes that indicate the size of a painting become L handshapes when the signer wants to show where to hang that painting.

The number handshapes carry very specific meaning in classifier predicates. In a conversation about how students filed into an auditorium, the signer will use the exact number handshape to represent the number of students who walked in at the same time. So, by changing the handshapes from 1 to 2 to 3, the signer changes the meaning of the predicate from *walk in single file* to *walk in two-by-two* to *walk in three-by-three*. Similarly, the signer will use 2 handshapes to show that two couples passed each other on the street, or 3 handshapes to show that chairs were arranged in groups of three.

ASL has many more classifier predicates than can be mentioned here. The important thing to remember is that classifier handshapes and movements can be combined in myriad ways. New classifier predicates are created as the language expands to represent new ideas and new technology. *The Gallaudet Dictionary of American Sign Language* features many examples of classifier predicates to illustrate the richness and vibrancy of ASL.

English Words That Are Usually Fingerspelled

The following words are usually fingerspelled as complete words or as abbreviations.

air = A-I-R
apartment = A-P-T
bank = B-A-N-K
bar = B-A-R
barbecue = B-B-Q
cab = C-A-B
car = C-A-R
ferry = F-E-R-R-Y
handicapped = H-C
headquarters = H-Q
heel = H-E-E-L
high school = H-S
ice = I-C-E
junior = J-R
liberal = L-I-B-E-R-A-L
map = M-A-P
menu = M-E-N-U
meter = M-E-T-E-R
mud = M-U-D
multiple sclerosis = M-S

nail = N-A I L
nap = N-A-P
news = N-E-W-S
oil = O-I-L
ounce = O-Z
pan = P-A-N
prescription = R-X
quarterback = Q-B
racquetball = R-B
rice = R-I-C-E
roll = R-O-L-L (bread)
rug = R-U-G
social security number = S-S + NUMBER
tablespoon = T-B-S (measure)
teaspoon = T-S-P (measure)
Total Communication = T-C
tip = T-I-P
toe = T-O-E
yard = Y-A-R-D

Dictionary *of* American Sign Language

abandon
forsake
leave
neglect

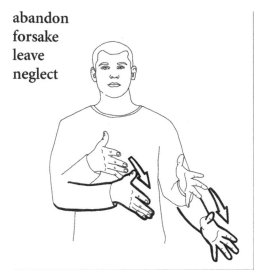

abbreviate
condense
summarize

a bit
little bit

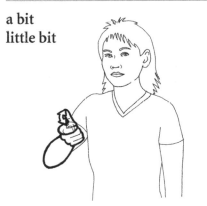

abortion

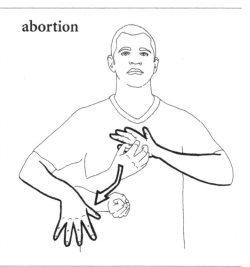

about
concerning
regarding

above
over

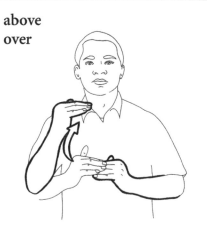

above

abuse
beat
hit

A/C (air conditioning)

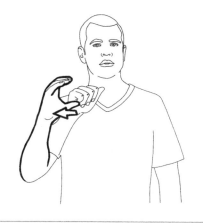

accept

accident (vehicle)
car accident
collision

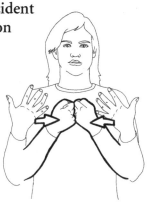

accident (vehicle)
car accident
collision

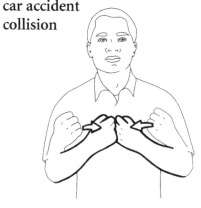

accident
mistake

accompany
go with

account
accounting

accuse

across
cross
over

act
perform

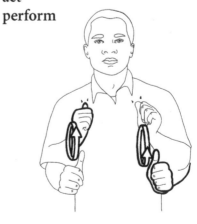

action
activity
deed

actor
actress

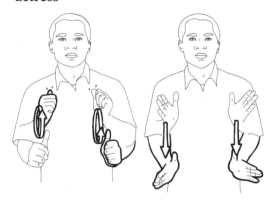

add
addition
additional
add-to
extra

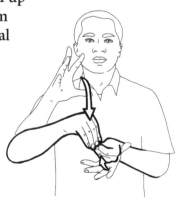

address
residence

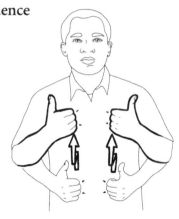

add up
sum
total

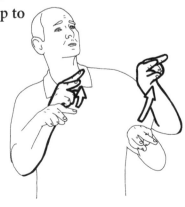

admire
look up to

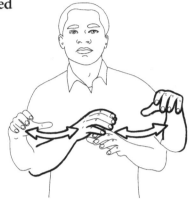

admission
entry

admit
confess
willing

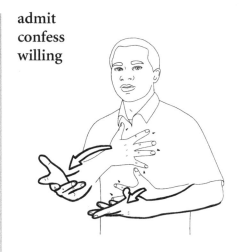

adopt
assume
take up

adult
grownup

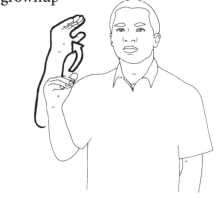

advertise
publicize

advertisement
ad
commercial

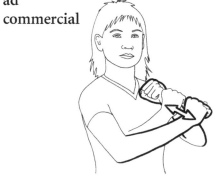

advice
counsel

advise

advisor
consultant
counselor

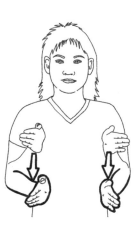

afraid
scare
scared
frighten
frightened
terrified
terrify

Africa

Africa

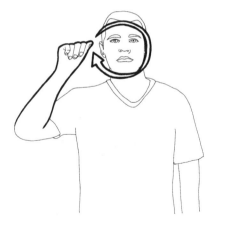

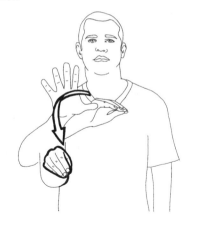

African American
black person

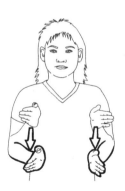

African American
black person

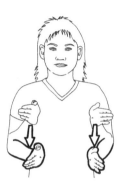

after
afterward
succession

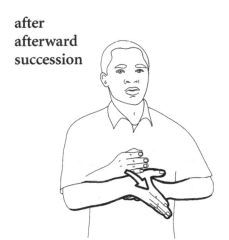

afternoon
P.M.

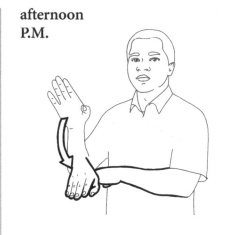

again
encore
over
repeat

again-again

age
old

aggravated

aggravated

agree
all in favor of
deal

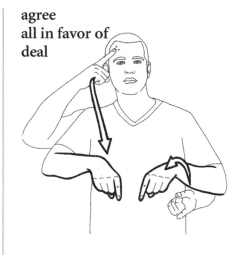

ahead

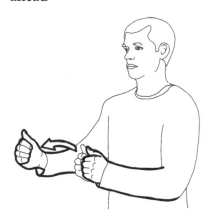

air
breeze

airplane
airport
pilot
plane

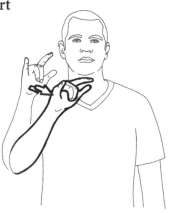

air pump

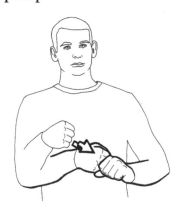

alarm

Alaska

alcohol
whiskey

alcoholic drink
cocktail
liquor

alcoholic drink
cocktail
liquor

algebra

all
entire
total
whole

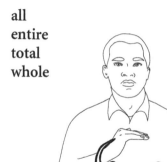

all (#ALL)

all day

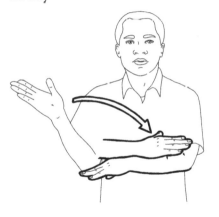

all gone
depleted
expired
run out of

alligator

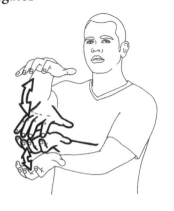

all night
overnight

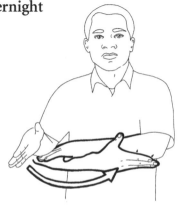

allow
grant
let
permit

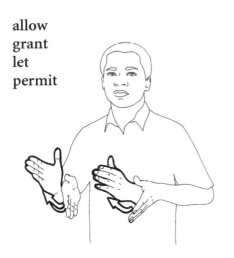

all right
okay

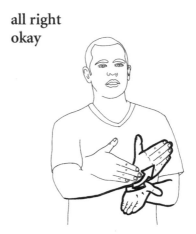

almost
nearly

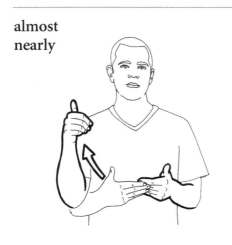

alone
isolated
lone
orphan

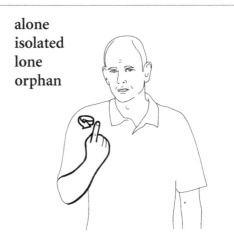

a lot
much

also
as well

Customer ID: *********2162

Items that you checked out

Title: John Wayne [videorecording] : the
ultimate collection
ID: 1110004649905
Due: Tuesday, July 5, 2022

Title: Colorado, rivers of the Rockies /
photography by John Fielder ; text
by Mark Pearson
ID: 1110004737551
Due: Monday, July 11, 2022

Title: Hearts aglow [sound recording] /
Tracie Peterson.
ID: 1110003376158
Due: Monday, July 11, 2022

Title: Ten patterns that explain the
universe / Brian Clegg
ID: 1110012022626
Due: Monday, July 11, 2022

Title: The Gallaudet Dictionary of
American Sign Language / Clayton
Valli.
ID: 1110012021289
Due: Monday, July 11, 2022

Title: The prepared home : how to stock,
organize, and edit your home to
thrive in comfort, safety, and sty
ID: 1110012023285
Due: Monday, July 11, 2022

Total Items: 6
Account balance: $0.00
6/27/2022 12:17 PM
Checked out: 13
Overdue: 0
Hold requests: 0
Ready for pickup: 0

Renew by phone: 249-9656

MONTROSE REGIONAL LIBRARY DISTRICT

www.montroselibrary.org • 970-249-9656

Customer ID: *********2162

Items that you checked out

Title: John Wayne [videorecording] : the
 ultimate collection.
ID: 1110004649905
Due: Tuesday, July 5, 2022

Title: Colorado, rivers of the Rockies /
 photography by John Fielder ; text
 by Mark Pearson.
ID: 1110004737551
Due: Monday, July 11, 2022

Title: Hearts aglow [sound recording] /
 Tracie Peterson.
ID: 1110003376158
Due: Monday, July 11, 2022

Title: Ten patterns that explain the
 universe / Brian Clegg.
ID: 1110012022626
Due: Monday, July 11, 2022

Title: The Gallaudet Dictionary of
 American Sign Language / Clayton
 Valli.
ID: 1110012021289
Due: Monday, July 11, 2022

Title: The prepared home : how to stock,
 organize, and edit your home to
 thrive in comfort, safety, and sty
ID: 1110012023285
Due: Monday, July 11, 2022

Total items: 6
Account balance: $0.00
6/27/2022 12:17 PM
Checked out: 13
Overdue: 0
Hold requests: 0
Ready for pickup: 0

Renew by phone: 249-9656

altogether

always
ever

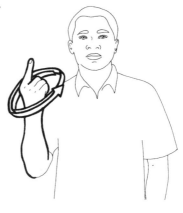

ambition

America

American Sign Language

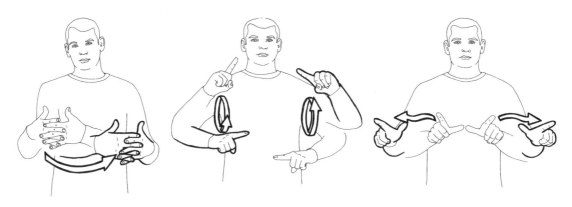

among

amount

Amsterdam

analyze
assess
evaluate
examine
gauge
investigate

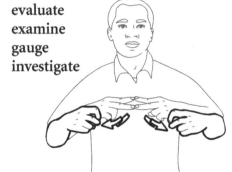

ancestors

ancient
former
historic
used-to

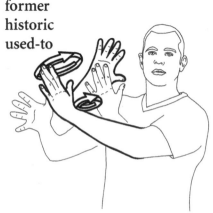

and

angel

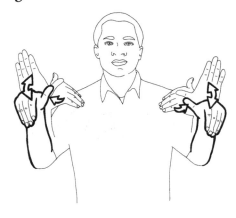

angry
anger
cross
furious
grouchy
grumpy
mad
rage

animal

announce
declare
proclaim

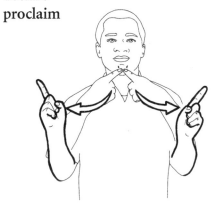

another
other

answer
reply
respond
response

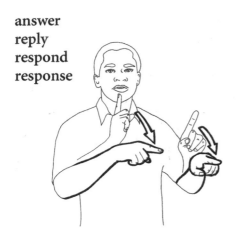

any

anyone
anybody

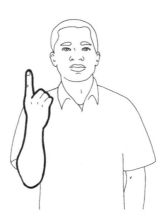

anything

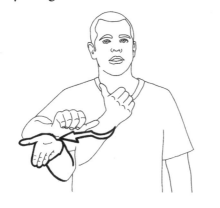

anywhere

appear
pop up
show up

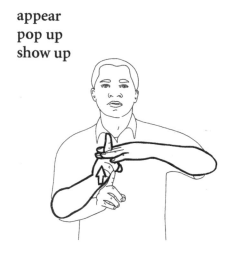

applaud (Deaf way)
commend
give an ovation
praise
wave
  hands

applaud (hearing way)
clap
commend
give an ovation
praise

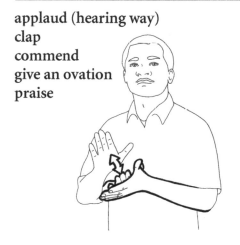

apple

apply
volunteer

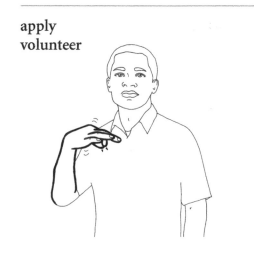

apply
use

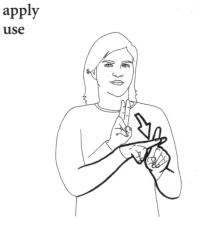

appoint

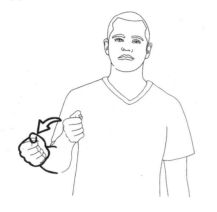

appointment
engagement

appointment
engagement

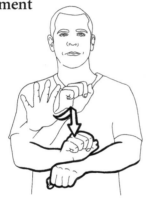

approach

appropriate
proper
suitable

approve
give seal of approval
seal
stamp

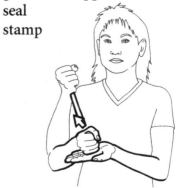

approximately
about
around

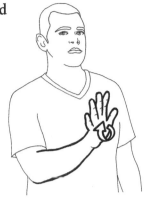

April Fool's Day

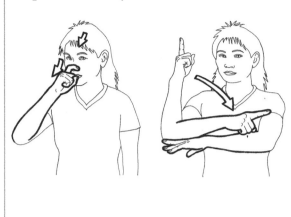

archery

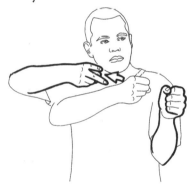

architecture

area
region
vicinity

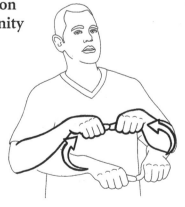

Argentina

arise
get up
stand up

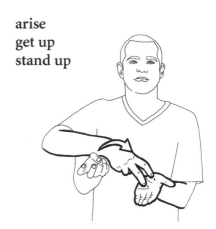

Arizona

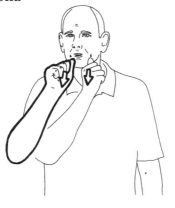

arm

around
orbit

arrive
reach

art

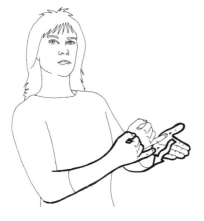

article

artist

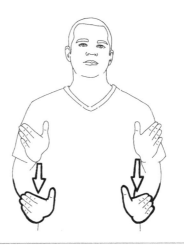

as

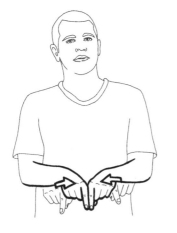

ashamed

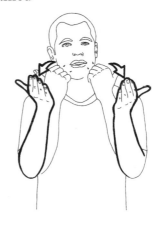

Asia

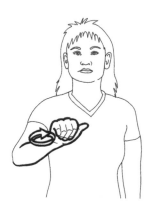

Asia

ask
request

ASL (American Sign Language)

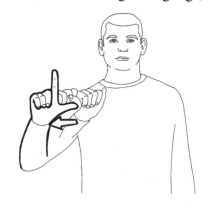

assist
aid
assistant

associate
each other
interact
mingle
mutual
socialize

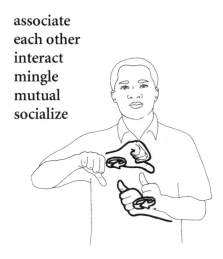

association
agency
fellowship

Athens

Atlanta

attempt
make an effort

attend
go

attendance

attention
focus

attitude

audience
congregation
crowd

audiologist

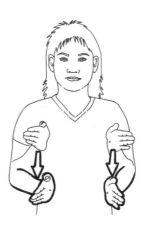

audiology

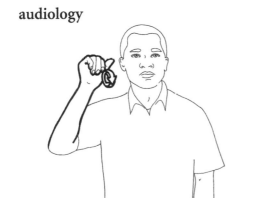

aunt

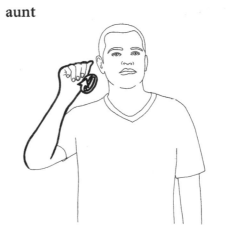

Australia

Australia

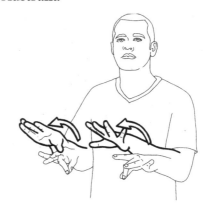

Austria

authority

average
mean
share

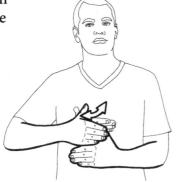

avoid

awake
awaken
arouse
wake up

award
trophy

away
get away

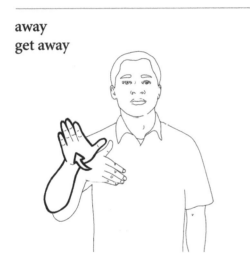

awful
dreadful
horrible
terrible

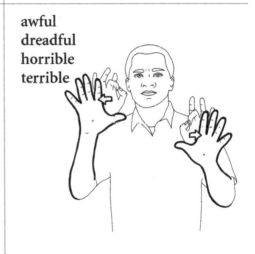

awkward
clumsy

baby
infant

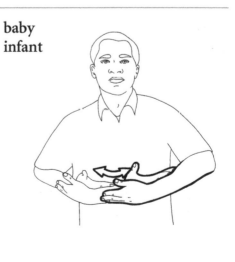

baby powder

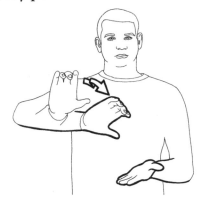

baby rattle

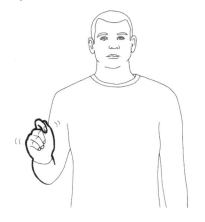

bachelor

back

back (#BACK)
return

background

back of one's mind

backpack

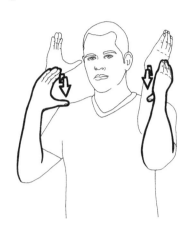

backstab
talk about people behind their back

back-together

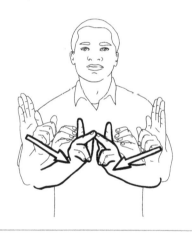

back-up
behind

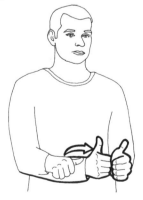

bacon

bad
naughty

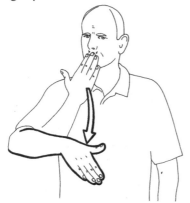

badge

badge

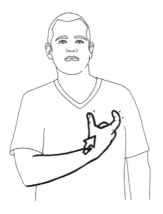

badminton

bag
basket
picnic
pot
sack
tank

bake
oven

baloney • 33

baking sprinkles

balance

bald

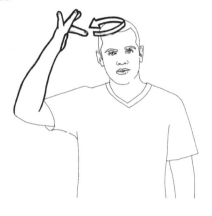

ball

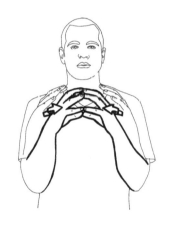

balloon

baloney
bologna
sausage

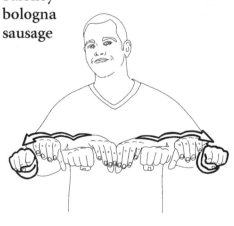

Baltimore

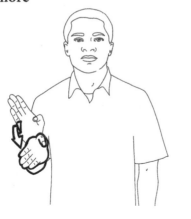

banana

band
orchestra

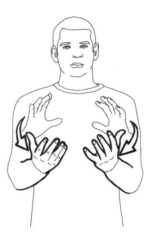

bandage
Band-Aid

Bangladesh

Baptist

bar

barber

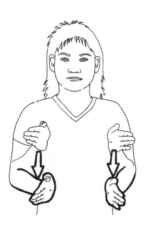

bark

baseball
softball

basement
cellar

basic
basis
underlying

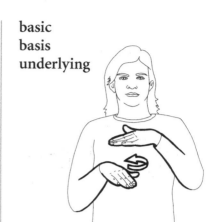

basket

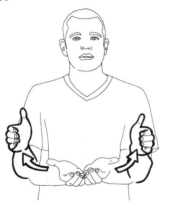

basket

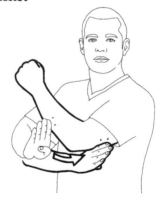

basketball

bat

bath
bathe

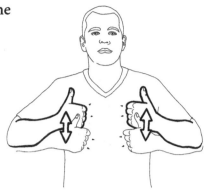

bathing suit

bathrobe

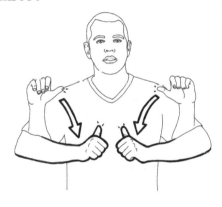

bathrobe (for men)

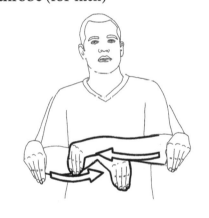

bathroom
toilet

bathtub

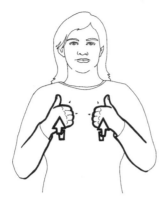 

bawl out
chew out
tell off
yell at

beach

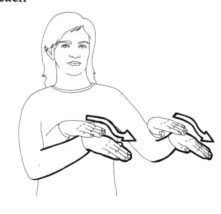

beans

bear

beard

beautiful

be careful
careful
exercise caution
take care
watch out

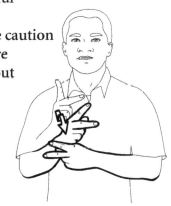

because
since

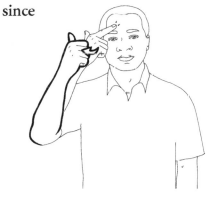

become
get

become fat
gain weight

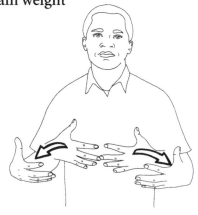

bed

bedroom

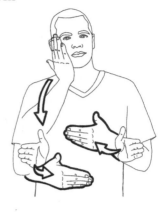

bee

beer

before
ago
past

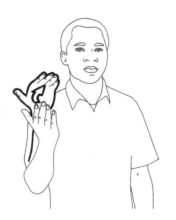

before
prior to

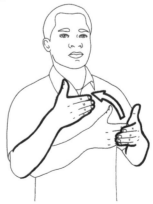

beg
plead

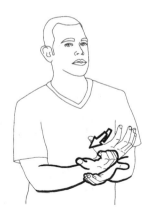

beggar

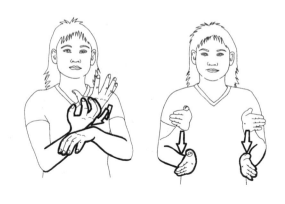

behave

behavior
conduct

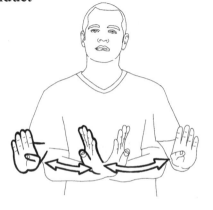

behind
avoid

Beijing

Belgium

Belgium

believe

Belize

bell

belong

belong

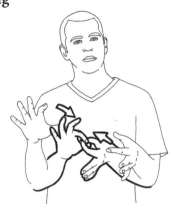

belong
truly yours

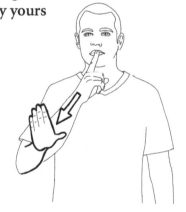

below
less than

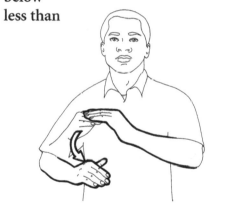

belt

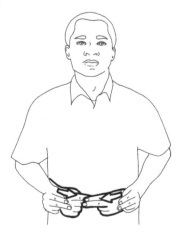

benefit
advantage
gain
profit

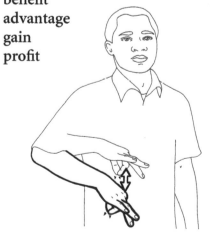

beside
next to

best

best friend
close friend
good friend

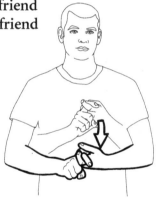

bet

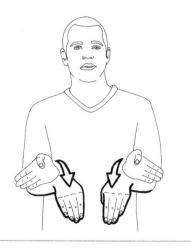

better

between
partner
share

beyond

Bible

bicycle
bike

bicycle pump

big
great
huge
large

bikini

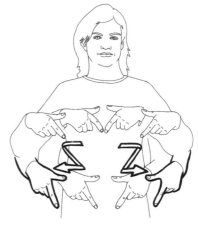

billion

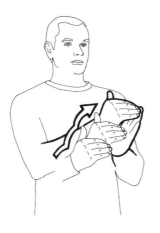

billionaire

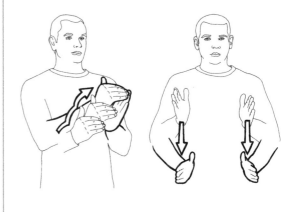

bind
tie-up

biology

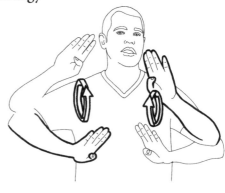

bird
chicken

birth
birthday

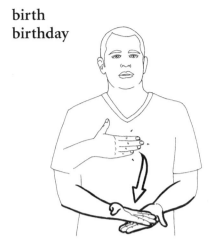

birthday

birthday

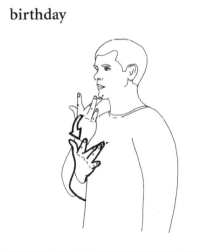

bison
buffalo

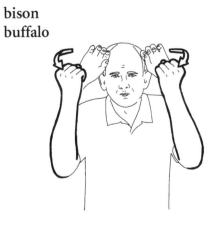

bite

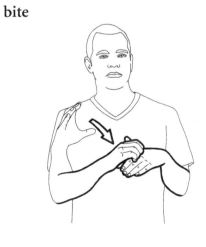

black

---

blackberry

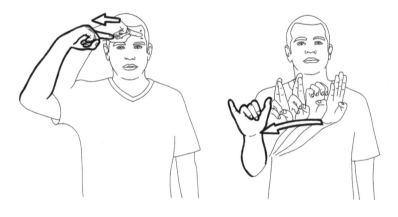

---

blame (noun)
accusation
fault

blame (verb)
accuse
charge

blanket

blank out

bless

blind

blind

blinds

blinds

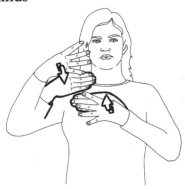

blink
wink

block
cube

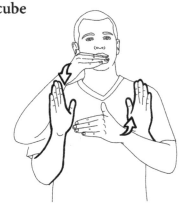

blockheaded

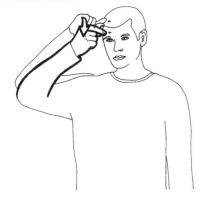

blond

blond

blood
bleed

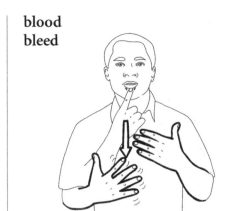

blossom (verb)
bloom

blouse

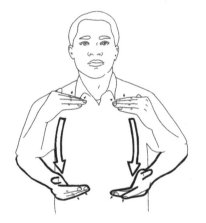

blow

blow nose

blow nose

blow up
blow one's top
temper

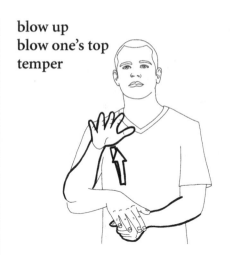

blue
navy

blueberry

 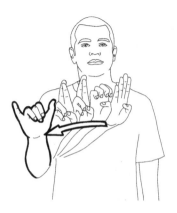

blush

boat

body

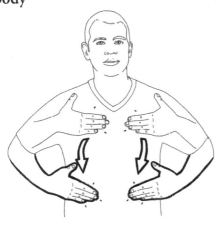

boil
burn

boiling mad
resentful
smoldering

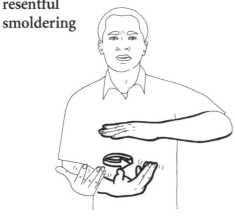

Bolivia

bomb

bomb

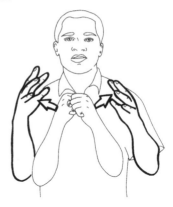

Bombay

book
album
textbook

boots

bored
boring
dry
dull
monotonous
tedious

born

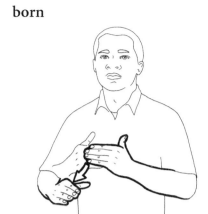

borrow

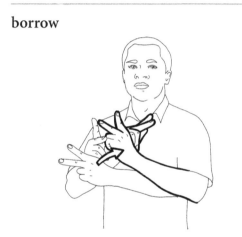

boss
chairperson

boss
chairperson
chief
VIP

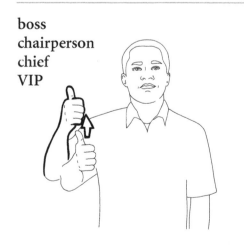

Boston

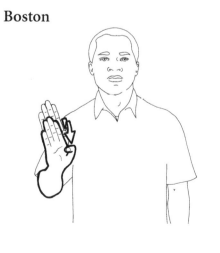

both

Botswana

bottle

bounce
dribble

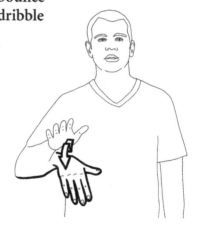

bowl

bowling

bowtie

bowtie

box
package

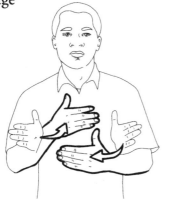

boxing

boxing

boy

boyfriend

bra	bracelet

 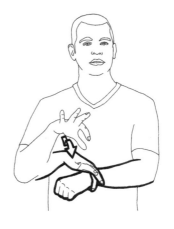

brag boast show off	brain mind

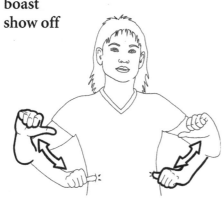 

brake

branch
fork in a road

branch (tree)

brave
courageous

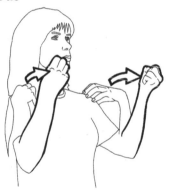

brawl
altercation

Brazil

bread

break
fracture

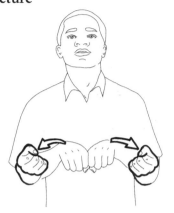

break
midday break

breakdown
collapse
cave-in

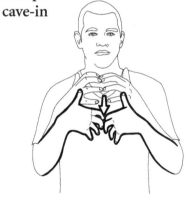

break down

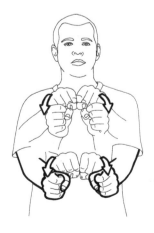

breakfast

breakfast

break a record

breasts

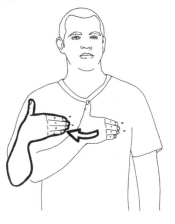

breathe

bridge

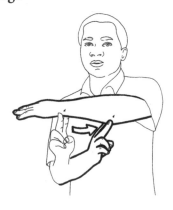

bring
deliver

broke

broom

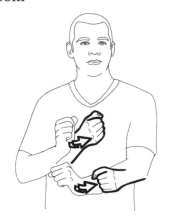

broom

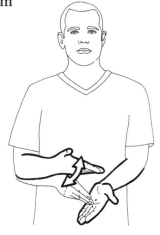

brother

brother

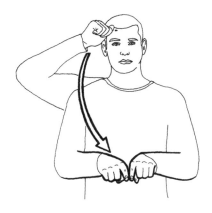

brother-in-law

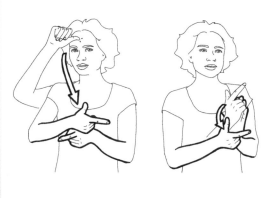

brown

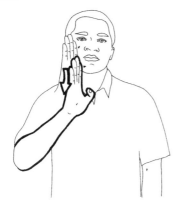

brushing teeth

bucket
pail

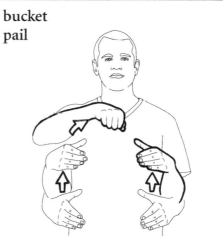

bug
insect

build
build-up
construct

building

building

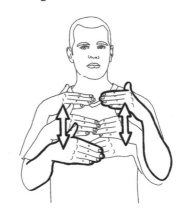

Bulgaria

bull

bull
nose ring

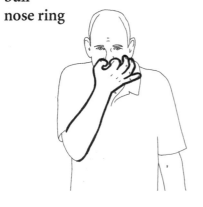

burn

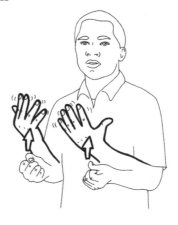

bury

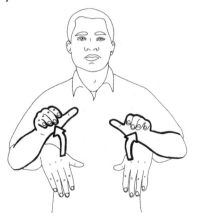

bus (#BUS)

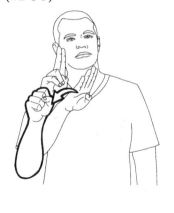

business

busy

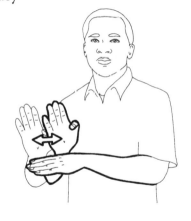

but
although
different
however
unlike

butter

butterfly

buttons

buy
purchase

bye
good-bye
wave good-bye

cabinet

cafeteria

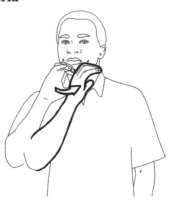

cake

calculus

calendar
chart
schedule

California

call on rotary telephone

call on telephone

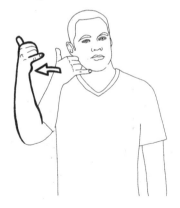

call on touch-tone telephone	call on TTY

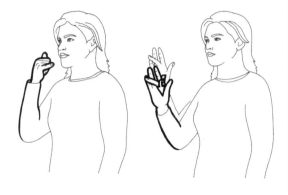 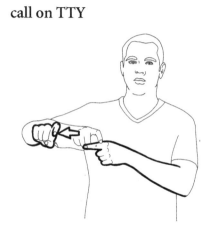

call out
roar
scream
shout
yell

camera

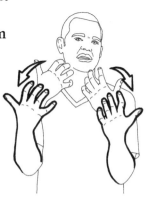 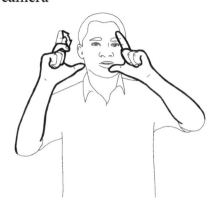

camping

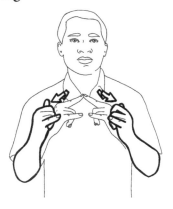

can
could

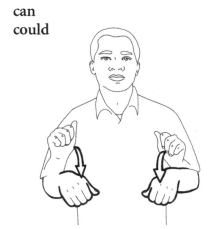

can
cup
glass
jar

Canada

candle

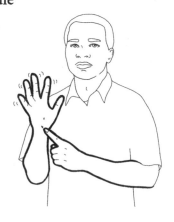

candy

candy

candy cane

cane

cannot
can't
couldn't
unable

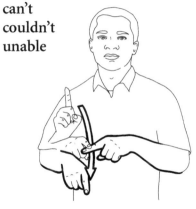

canoe

canoeing (verb)
kayaking
rowing

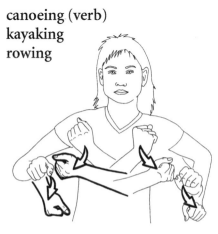

can't forget something painful
can't get something difficult off
  one's mind
mental scar

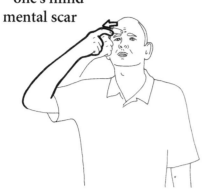

capital (city)
captain

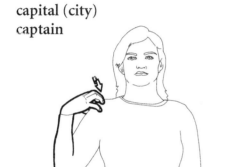

capital letter

capitol
government seat

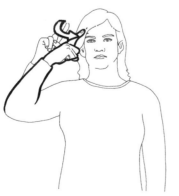

captions
closed captions
subtitles

capture
apprehend
arrest
catch

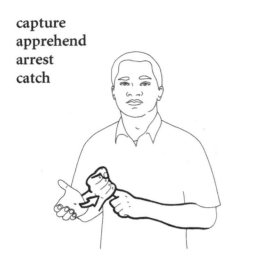

car
automobile
vehicle

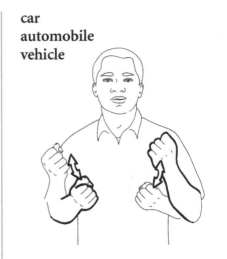

car dashboard
dash

careless
reckless

car engine

carpenter
woodworker

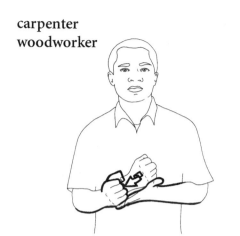

carrot

carry

cashier

cassette tape
tape recording

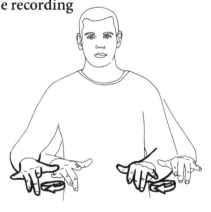

cat

catch
apprehend
nab

catch
catch ball

caterpillar

Catholic

Caucasian (person)
white person

cause

ceiling

celebrate
anniversary
celebration
festival
holiday
victory

cent
one cent
penny

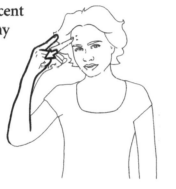

center
central
middle

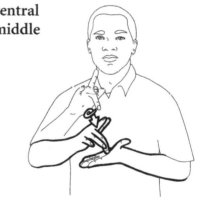

center
central
middle

Central America

cereal

certificate
certification

certify

chain

chair
seat

chalk

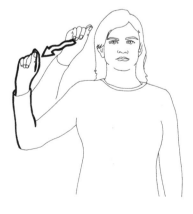

challenge
play against

champagne

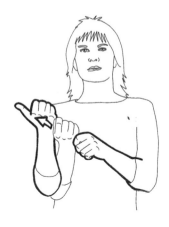

champion

chance

change
adapt
adjust
alter
modify

change
(money)

channel

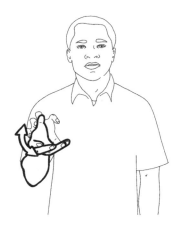

chapter

character (individual)

character (personality)

charge
cost
fare
fee
fine
price
tax

Charlotte (NC)

chase

chat

cheap
inexpensive

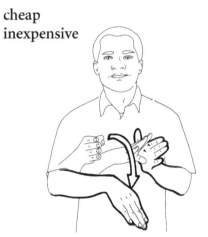

cheat

cheat

cheat

check
approve
inspect

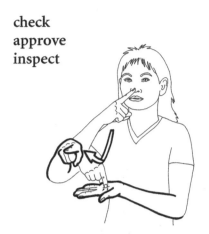

checkers

checking account

check mark
check off (a list)

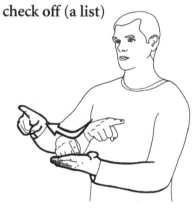

cheek

cheese

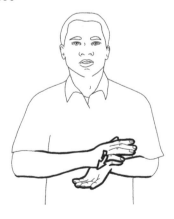

chef
cook (noun)

 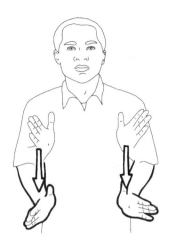

chemistry
chemical

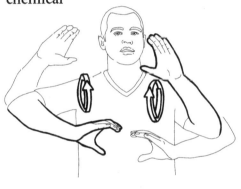

cherry

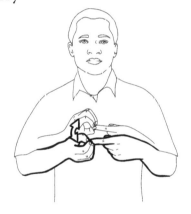

chest

chew

chewing gum
gum

Chicago

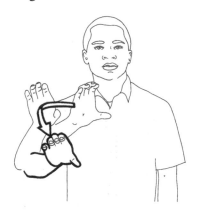

child

children

Chile

chin

China

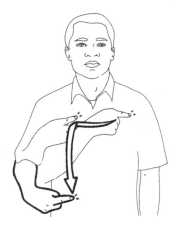

China

chocolate
cocoa

choice

choices

choke (oneself)

choke (another person)

choose
select

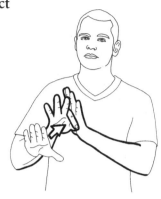

choose
pick

Christian

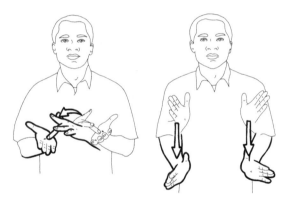

Christmas

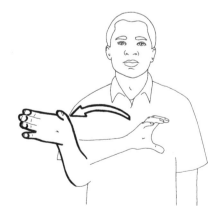

chuckle

church
chapel

cigar

cigarettes

circle
orbit
round

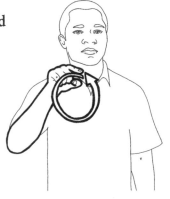

circumcise

circus
clown

cited
get a ticket

city
downtown
uptown

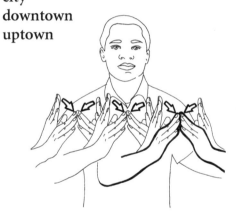

class

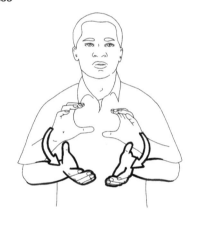

classroom

clean
nice
neat
pure
tidy

clean-up

clear
bright
light

climb

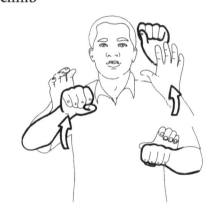

clip bushes

clip nails

clip nails

---

clock

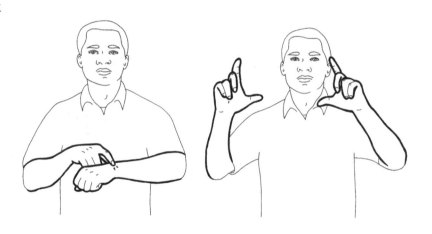

---

close
shut

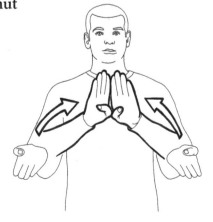

close (door)

close
near

closer
nearer

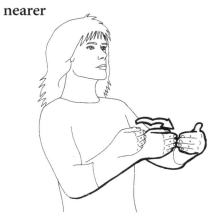

close window
shut window

closet

clothes
apparel
garments

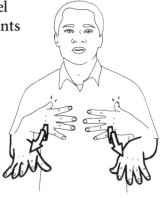

clouds

coach

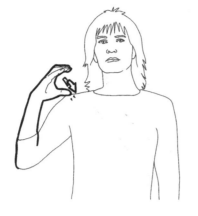

coat
jacket
overcoat

cocktail

coconut

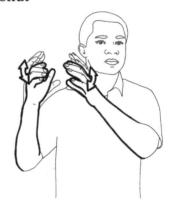

coffee

coins

Coke

cold (illness)
head cold

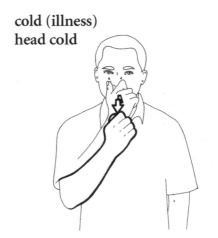

cold (temperature)
chilly
frigid
winter

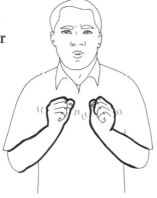

collapse
breakdown

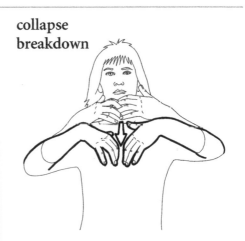

collar

collect
accumulate
amass
gather
reap

collection
earnings
income
salary
wages

college

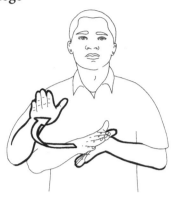

Colombia

color

Colorado

Colorado

comb

comb hair (verb)

come

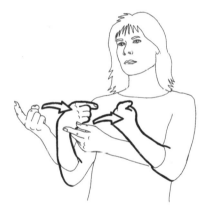

come

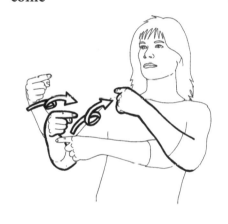

come here

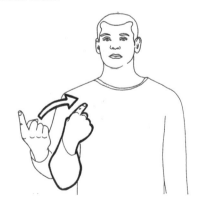

come-on

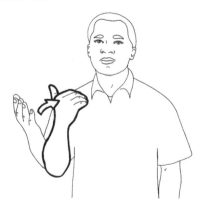

comfortable
comfort

command
direct
order

commandments

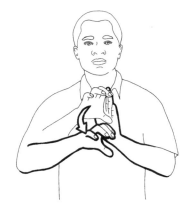

committee
Congress

communicate
communication
conversation
converse

Communist

community
town

commute
go back and forth

company (#CO)

company
guests

compare
comparison

compete
competition
run

complain
complaint

complete
full

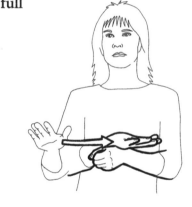

computer

computer

concept

concerned

conclusion

conduct (music)

conductor (music)

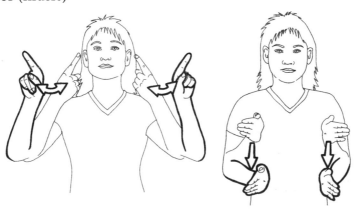

conductor (train)

confident
confidence
trust

conflict
clash
contradict

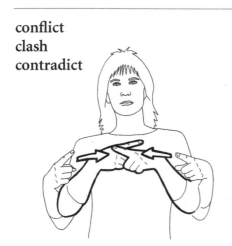

confuse
confusing

confused
mixed-up

congratulate
congratulations

connect
attach
join

conquer
beat
defeat
overcome

consider
think about

consistent

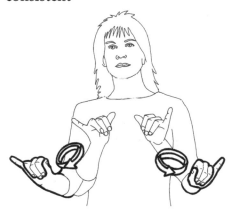

constant
consistent

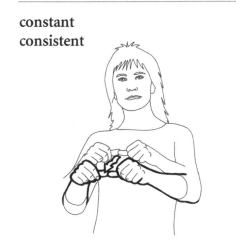

constant
even

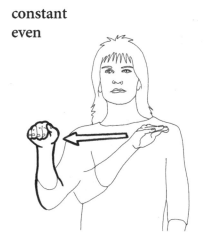

Constitution

consume
devour

consumer
customer
shopper

 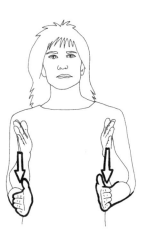

consumer
customer
user

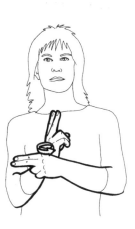 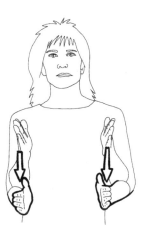

contact

contact lenses

continue
endure
last
lasting
move on
permanent

control
direct
govern
manage
manipulate
regulate
reign
rule
run (chair a
    meeting)

convince
persuade

cook (verb)
cooking
fry

Note: Use a K handshape to sign *kitchen*.

cookie

cooperate
cooperation

copy
ape
duplicate
imitate
parrot

copy (machine)
xerography
xerox

corn

corn
corn on the cob

corner

corner

correct (verb)
cancel

correspondence
letters

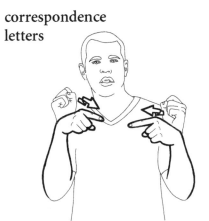

Costa Rica

couch

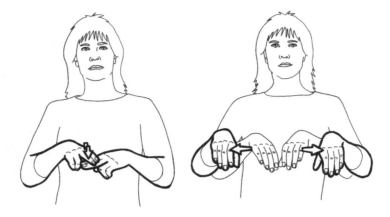

cough

cough

count
figure

country
land

country

couple
pair
partners

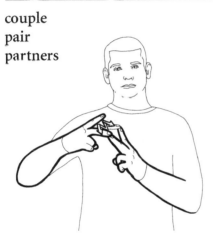

course
chapter

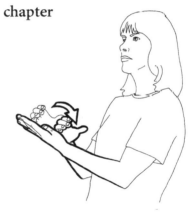

court
justice
trial

courthouse

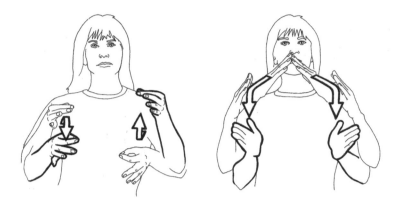

cousin

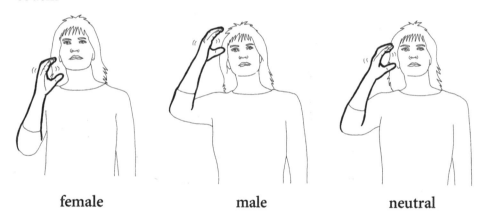

female   male   neutral

cover (verb)

cover-up (verb)
hide

cow
cattle

CP (cerebral palsy)

crack

cracker
Passover

crash

crawl
baby crawling

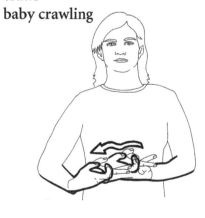

crawl

crazy
wow!

crazy

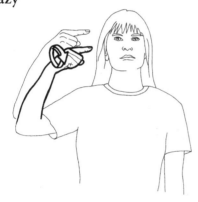

crazy
wild

crazy for
wild about

crazy for

cream

credit card

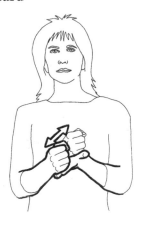

creek
stream

crippled
lame

criticize

cross (noun)
crucifix

crowd
horde

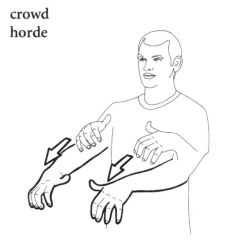

crowded
crushed

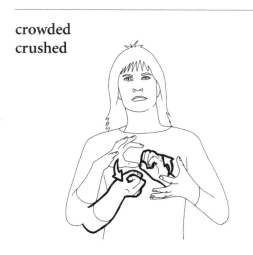

crown

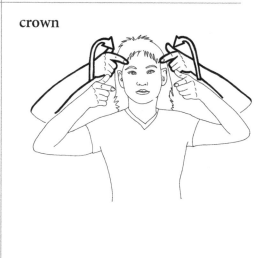

crown

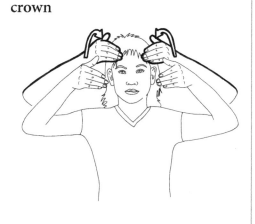

crush
crumble
grind
mash

crutches

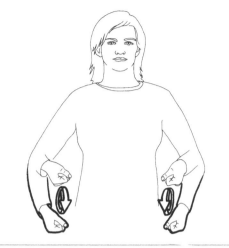

cry
cry a lot
weep

cry

Cuba

culture

cut fabric

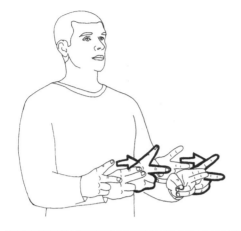

cut paper

cute

cycle

Dallas

dance

danger
dangerous
peril
risk
unsafe

dare

dare
I challenge you

dark
shadow

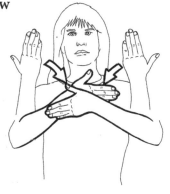

dart

dash
hurry off
leave
scoot
take off

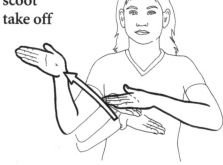

dash
short line

date

daughter

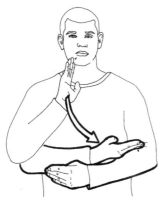

daughter

day

dead
death

deaf

deaf

deal cards
play cards

debate
discuss

debt (noun)
due
owe (without
    repeat
    movement)

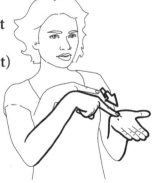

deceive
betray

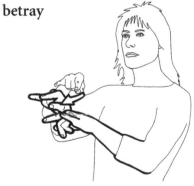

decide
decision
determine
make up
   one's mind

decide
decision
determine
make up
   one's mind

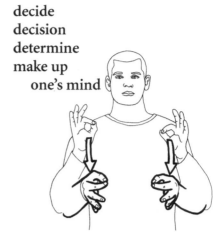

decorate
elaborate

deep
depth
detail
in depth

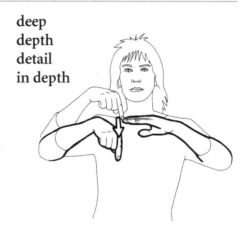

deer

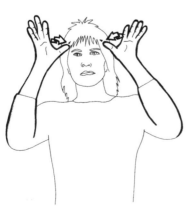

defend
protect

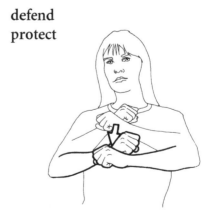

deflate
diminish

deflate partially

delicious
tasty

demand
insist
require

Democrat

demonstrate
give an
     example

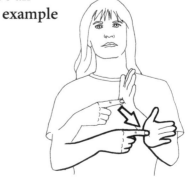

demonstration
example
symbol

Denmark

dentist

deny

department

depend

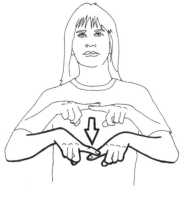

dependable
count on
rely on

deposit

depressed
dejected
discouraged

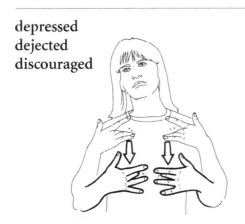

depressed
dejected
discouraged

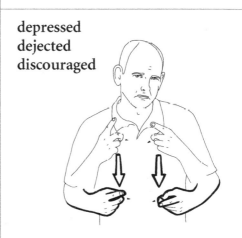

desert

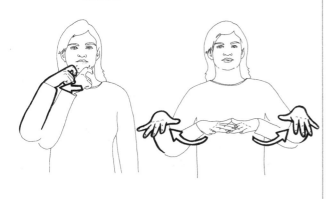

design

dessert

destroy
damage
demolish

detective

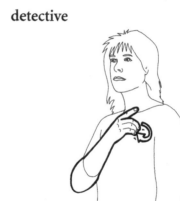

detergent
laundry soap

deteriorate
diminish

deteriorate
diminish

Detroit
Denver

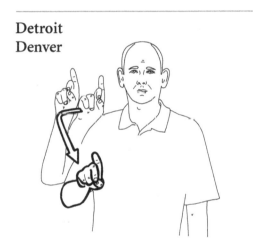

develop
development

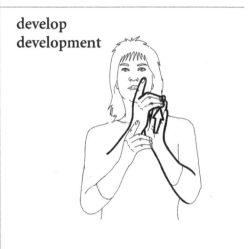

develop
climax
peak

devil
demon
evil
mischief
mischievous
Satan
wicked

dialogue
converse
talk

diamond

dictator

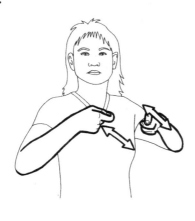 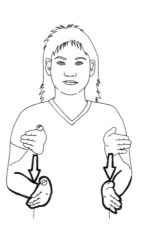

dictionary

diet

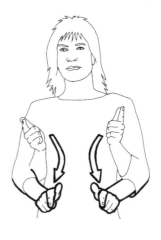

difficult
difficulty

dig

dim
turn down
  lights

dime
ten cents

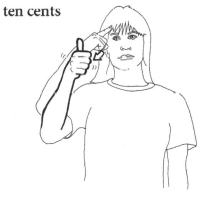

dimples

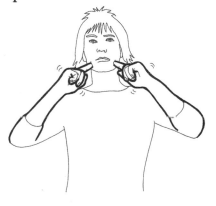

dining room

dining room

dinner

dinner

dinosaur

diploma
degree

diploma

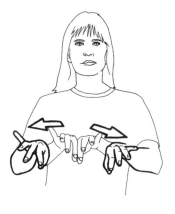

direction

director

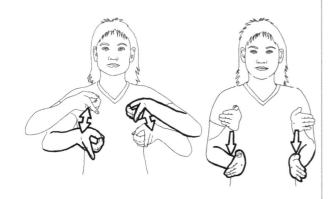

dirt
ground
land
sand
soil

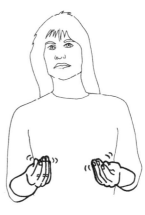

dirty

disagree

disappear (verb)
vanish

disappoint
disappointed

discipline

disconnect
detach
release
turn loose

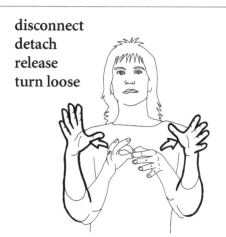

discontented
dissatisfied
unsatisfied

discrimination

discuss
discussion

disgust
revulsion

dish
plate
saucer

dish
plate
saucer

dismiss
discharge
excuse
exempt
lay off
waive

disobey
disobedience
protest
rebel
revolt
strike

distribute
disseminate
scatter
spread

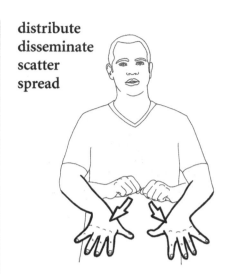

disturb
annoy
bother
interfere

disturbed
emotionally disturbed

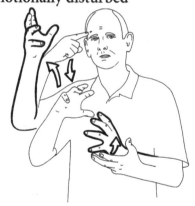

dive

dive

divide
split

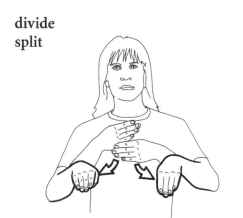

divorce
divorced

dizzy

do
act
behave

doctor
physician

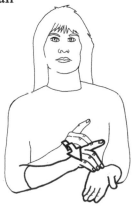

doctor
physician

dog

doll
toy

dollar

dollar

Dominican Republic

Dominican Republic

donkey

don't

don't care
don't mind

don't care

don't know
unknown
unsure

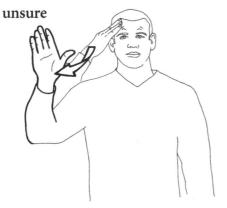

don't like
dislike

don't want

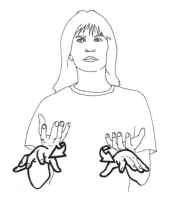

door

doorbell

dormitory

double
twice

doubt
don't believe
skeptical
unsure

doughnut

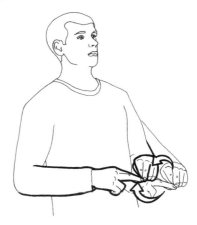

down

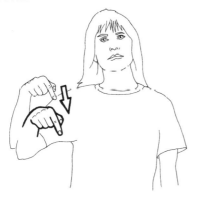

downstairs

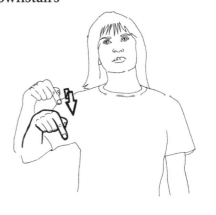

do work

Do you mind?

drag
pull

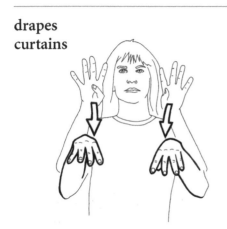

drama
performance
play
show
theater

drapes
curtains

draw
illustrate

drawing
illustration

dream
fantasize

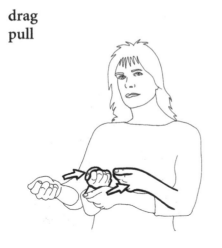

dress (noun)
fashion

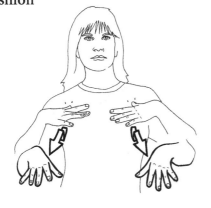

dress (verb)

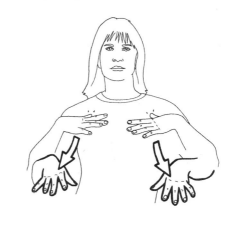

dresser
drawers

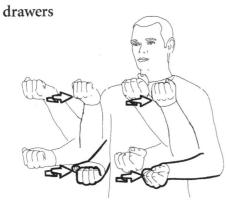

dresser
drawers

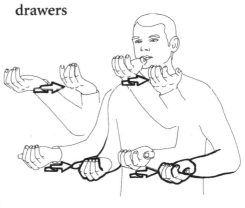

drill (noun)

drink
beverage

drip
slow leak

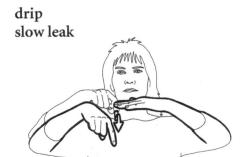

drive

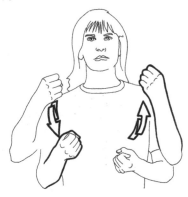

drive-to

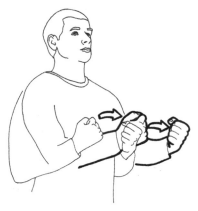

drop (verb)
dump

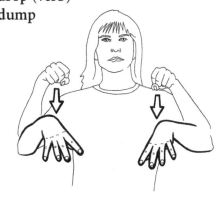

drops (noun)

drown

drown

drugs
illicit substances

drugs
medicine

drums

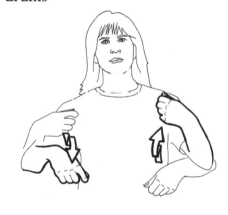

drunk

dry

dryer

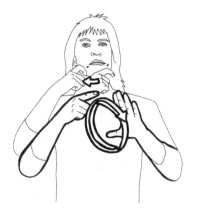

dryer

Dublin

duck

during
while

dust (verb)
wipe

duty

dye

each
apiece
every

eager
ambitious
anxious
earnest
enthusiastic
motivated
zealous

eagle

ear

earache

early

early (#ELY)

ear muffs
ear phones

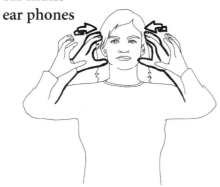

earrings

earth
geography

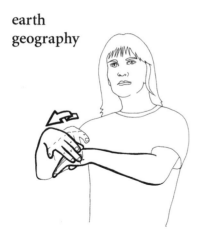

earthquake

east

Easter

easy

eat
dine

economy
economics

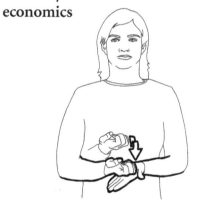

Ecuador

edge

education

effort

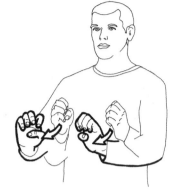

egg

ego

Egypt

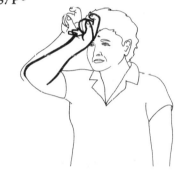

eight

eight cents

eighteen (formal)

eighteen (informal)

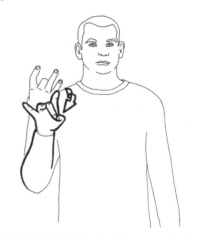

either

elastic
stretchy

elbow

election

electrician

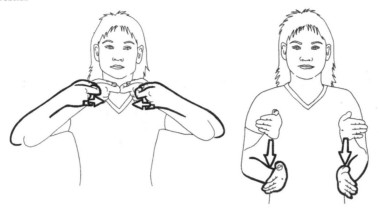

electricity
electric

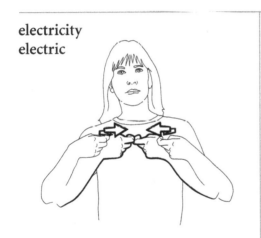

elementary
basic

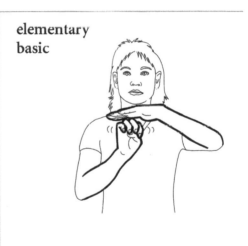

elephant

elevator

eleven

eliminate
delete

El Salvador

e-mail

embarrassed

emergency

emotion

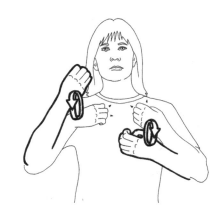

emphasize
emphasis
impress
stress

empty
available
bare
blank
space
vacant

encounter
approach
confront
face

encourage
coax
persuade

encyclopedia

encyclopedia

end
complete
last

enemy
foe
opponent
rival

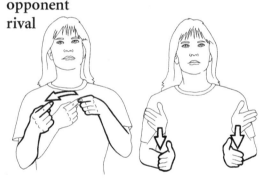

energy

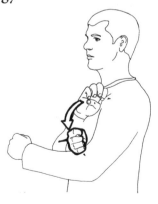

engaged

engagement

engineer
engineering

England (ASL)
English (language)

England (British)

enjoy
appreciate
enjoyable
enjoyment
like
take pleasure in

enough
adequate
sufficient

enter
entrance
go into
into

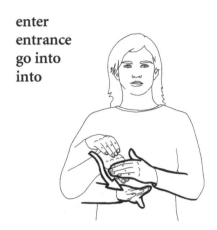

envelope
bank check

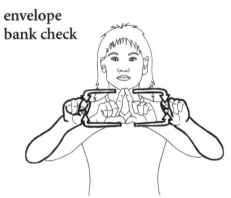

environment

Episcopal

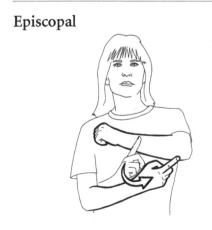
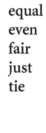

equal
even
fair
just
tie

equipment

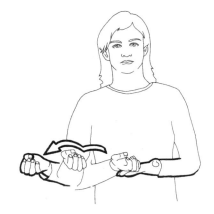

erase

erase

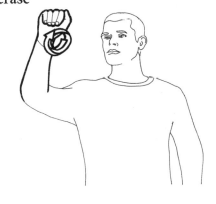

escape
flee
get away
run away

establish
base
found
set up

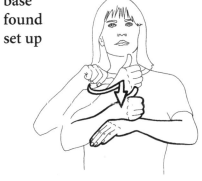

et cetera

Europe

evaluate

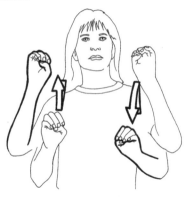

evening

event
excite
thrill
what's up?

everyday
daily

every Friday

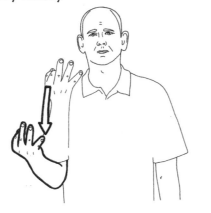

every Monday

everyone
everybody

everyone
everybody

every Saturday

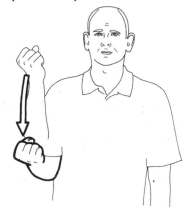

every Sunday

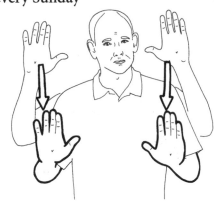

everything

every Thursday

every Thursday

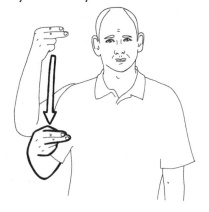

every Tuesday

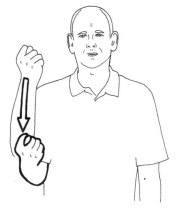

every Wednesday

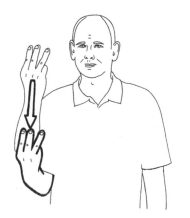

everywhere

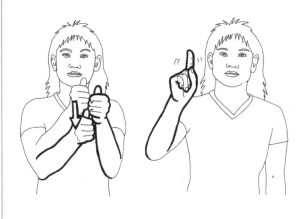

exact
accurate
just
precise
specific

exact
accurate
just
precise
specific

exaggerate
elaborate

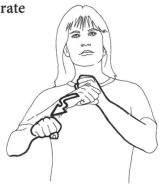

exams
examinations

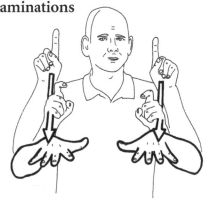

exceed

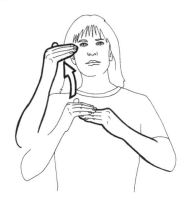

exchange
replace
return
substitute
trade
trade in

exciting
excited
excitement

excuse (noun)

excuse me

exercise

exercise

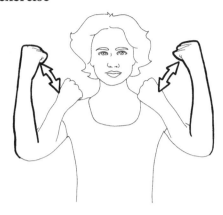

expand

expensive
costly

experience

experiment

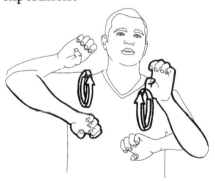

expert
good-at
proficient
skill
skilled
talent
talented

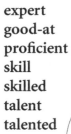

expert
good-at
proficient

explain
explanation

express
expression

eyebrow

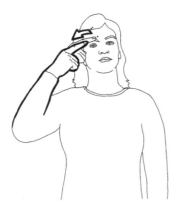

eyelashes

eye patch
pirate

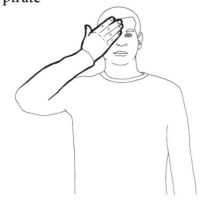

eyes

face
appearance

facial expression

fail

faint

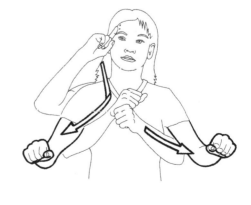

fair
so-so

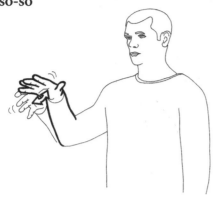

fair
fairly

faith

faithful

fall (verb)

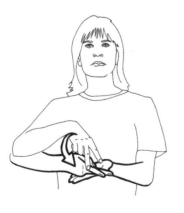

fall (noun)
autumn

fall in love

false
artificial
counterfeit
fake
imposter
pseudo

family

famous

fancy
elegant
luxury
prim
proper

fantasy (noun)

far
distant

farm

farmer

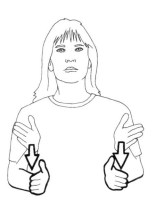

fast
immediate
quick
rapid
speedy
swift

fast (verb)
fasting

fat (derogatory sign)

fat
chubby
obese
overweight

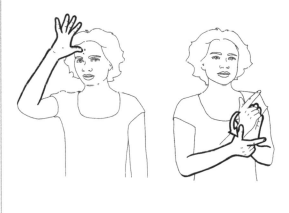

father
dad

father-in-law

fault

fax
facsimile

fear
fearful

feast
feasting

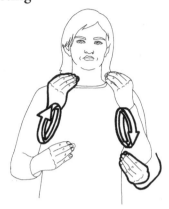

federal

feed

feel
feelings
sensation
sense

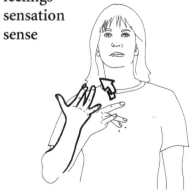

feet

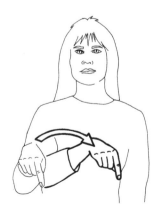

figure • 167

fence

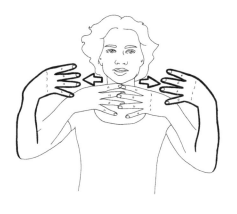

fifteen

fifth
five dollars

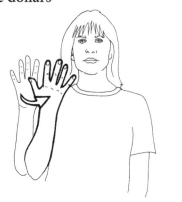

fight (verb)
fighting

fight (noun)
statistics

figure (noun)
shape

file (noun)

file (verb)

fill out form

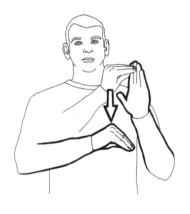

fill up gas tank

filthy
messy

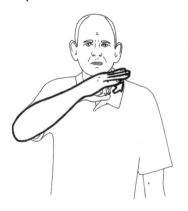

finally
at last
pah!

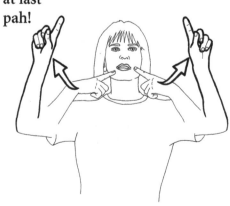

financial
finances

find
discover
locate

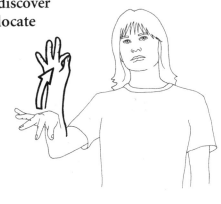

fine
well

finger

fingerprints

fingers

fingerspelling (noun)
spelling

fingerspelling (verb)

finish
already
complete
did
done
over
through

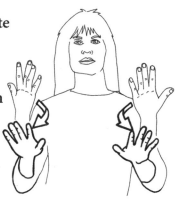

Finland

fire (noun)
flames

fired
dismissed
let go

firefighter

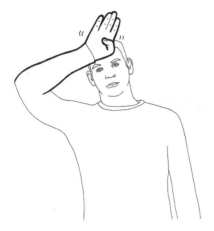

fireplace

first
original

fish

fishing

fishing net

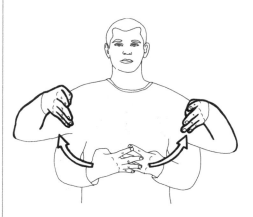

fist

fit

five

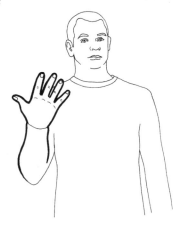

fix

fix (#FX)

flag

flag

flashing lights

flashlight

flashlight

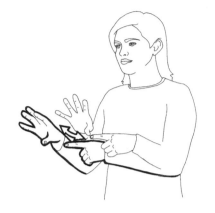

flat

flat tire

flexible

flexible

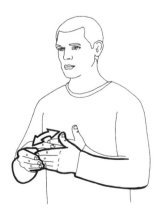

flip over

flip paper over

flipping out
freaking out
going crazy
losing one's mind

flirt
philander

float

flood

floor

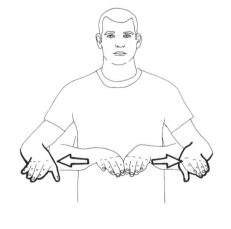

Florida (#FLA)

flow
flowing water

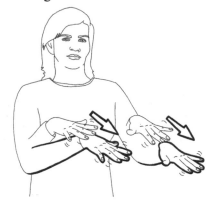

flow
fluent
skilled
smooth

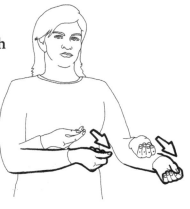

flower

flunk

flute

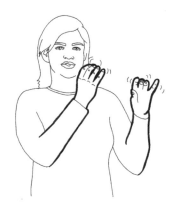

fly (verb)
bird flying

fly a kite

fly an airplane
airplane flying

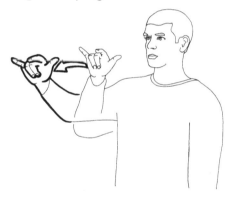

fold

follow (verb)
go after
pursue
track

fond

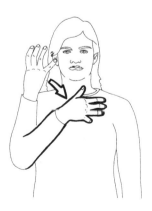

foreign
country

foreign

forest
jungle
woods

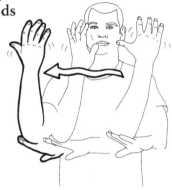

forever
eternal
everlasting

forget
because

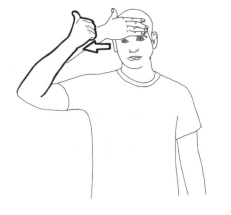

forgive
pardon

forgive me

fork

fork

form

form

Fort Worth

forty

foul up plans

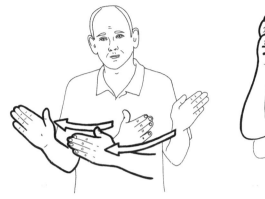 

foundation	four
	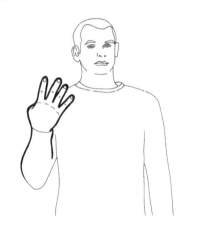

fourteen	fox

frame

France
French

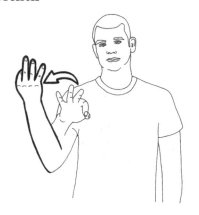

freckles

free
freedom
liberty

freeze
freezer
frozen

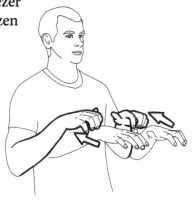

french fries

freshman

freshman

freshman

Friday

friend
friendship

friendly
pleasant

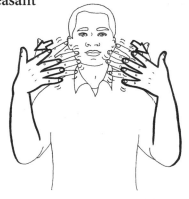

frog

from

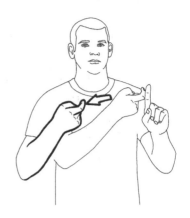

from now on

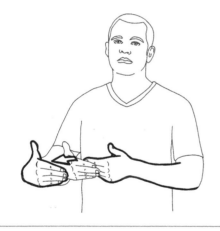

front

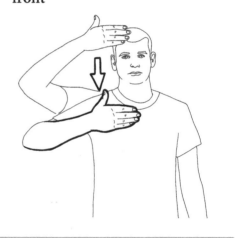

frown

frown

fruit

frustrated

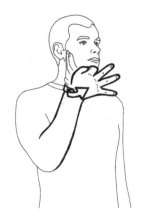

frustrated

full
complete
filled

full (of food)
sated
satisfied

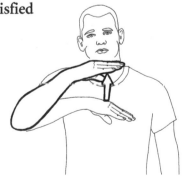

full
fed up

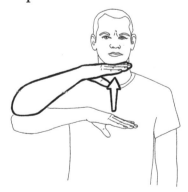

fun
leisure
recreation

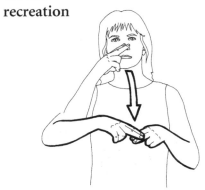

function

funeral

funny
amusing
humorous

furniture

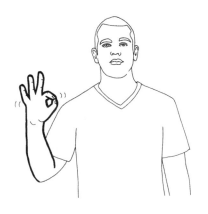

future
someday
will

Gallaudet

gamble
dice

game

gang
street gang

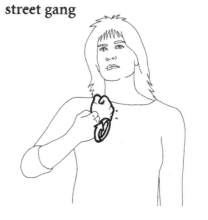

gang
group of friends

garage

garbage
refuse
trash
waste

gardening

gasoline (noun)

gate

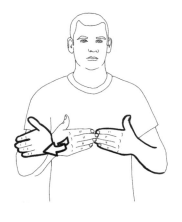

gay
homosexual

general

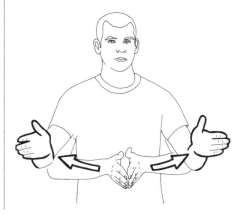

generation

gentle
kind

gentleman

geometry

Germany
(ASL)

Germany
(German)

get
acquire
catch
obtain
receive

get along
go along
move on

get in

get on

get out
take a hike

get rid of
throw out

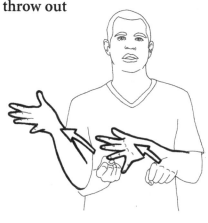

get up

ghost
spirit

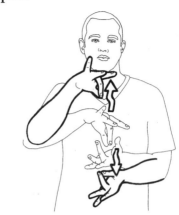

giant
big
enormous
huge

giant
tall

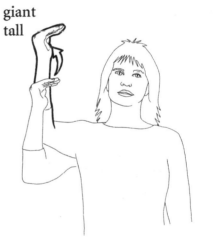

gift
present

giggle

giraffe

girl
female

girlfriend

give
contribute
contribution
grant

give

give up
sacrifice
surrender

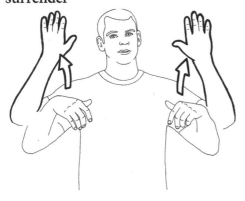

glance
look briefly

glance
notice something

glare

glass
material

glasses
spectacles

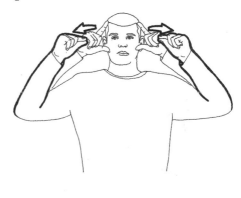

globe

glory

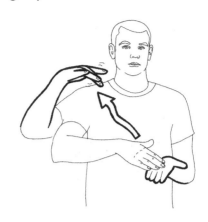

gloves

glue (noun)

glue (verb)

go
went

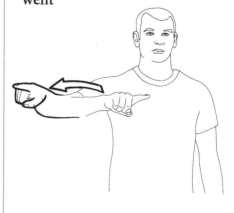

go ahead
go on
move on
proceed

go away
get away

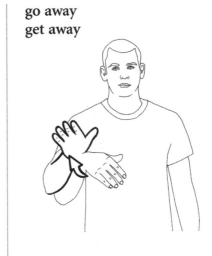

go by boat

go by subway

go by train

goal
objective

goat

God

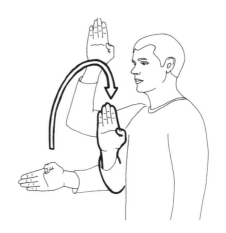

gold

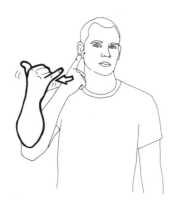

golf

gone
absent
missing

good
benevolent
well

good at
skilled

good luck
thumbs-up

good luck
thumbs-up

good morning

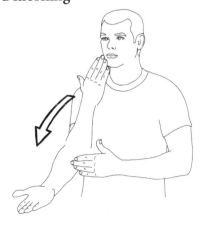 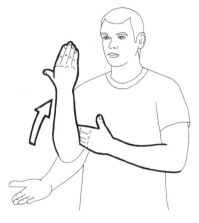

good morning

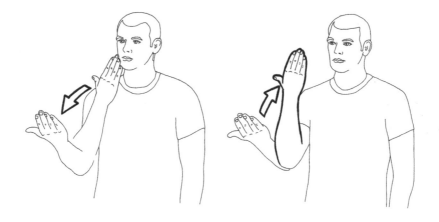

good night

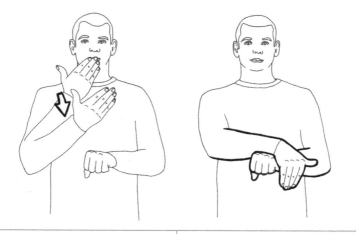

gossip
rumor

go steady
steady date

go to it!

government

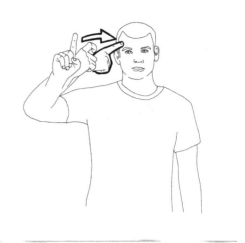

governor

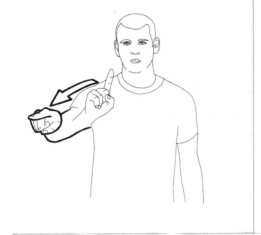

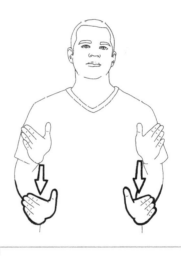

grab

grab opportunity

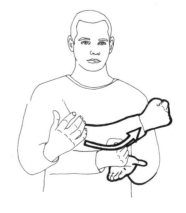

graduate (verb)

graduate student (noun)

grammar

grandfather
grandpa

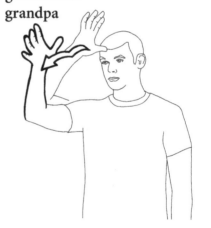

grandmother
grandma

grapes

grass
hay

gravy
grease
greasy
oil
oily

gravy
grease
greasy
oil
oily

gray

Greece (ASL)
Greek

Greece (Greek)
Greek

green

greet
hi

grief
sorrow
sorrowful

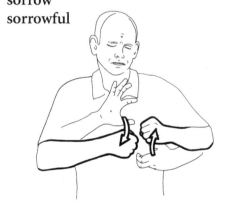

grip

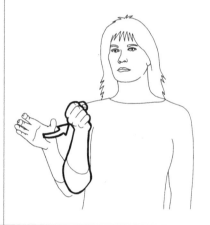

grocery store
food store

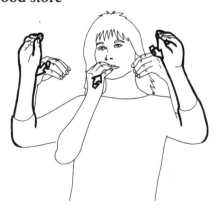

grouchy
grumpy

group
order

group
community

grow

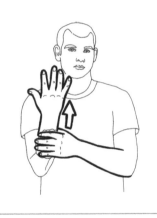

grow up
raise (a child)

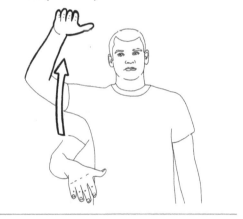

guardian
caretaker
custodian

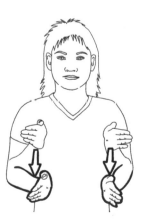

Guatemala

guess
assume
estimate
miss

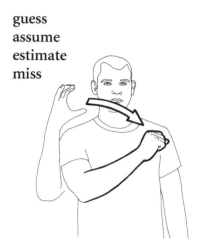

guide
lead

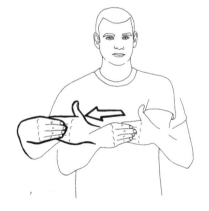

guilt
apprehensive

guilty

guitar

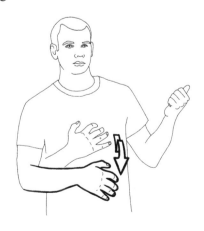

guitar

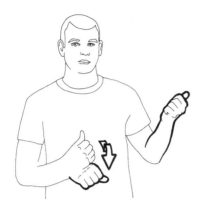

gun
pistol

gym

gym

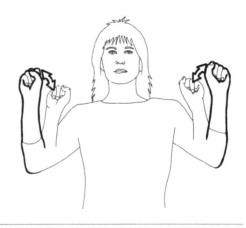

habit
accustom
custom

hair

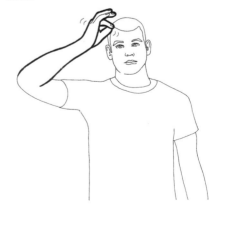

hairbrush
brush

Haiti

Haiti

hall
hallway

hall (#HALL)

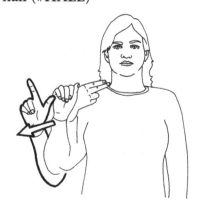

Halloween

Halloween

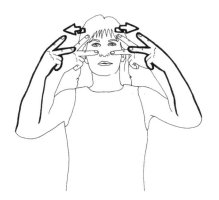

Hamburg

hamburger
burger

hammer

handkerchief
tissue

hands

handsome

hanger

hang up clothes

hang up phone

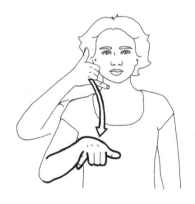

Hanukkah

happen
circumstance
coincide
incident
occur

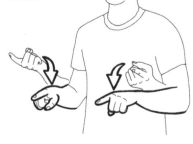

happy
cheer
cheerful
content
glad
merry

hard
difficult

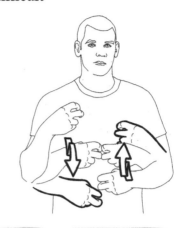

hard of hearing

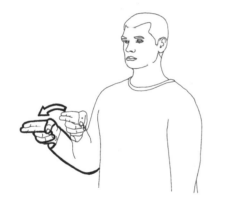

harp

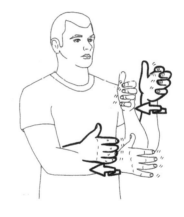

harvest
crops
gather

hat

hate
abhor
despise
detest
loathe

have
has
had
own
possess

have to

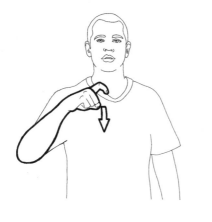

Hawaii

he
her
him
she

head

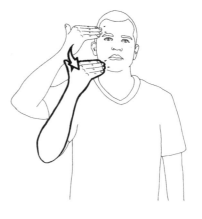

headache

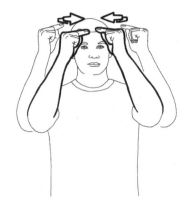

headline

heal
get well
health
healthy
well

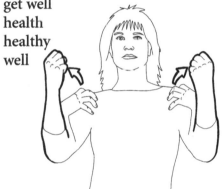

hearing (person)
public

hearing aid (behind the ear)

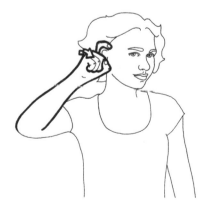

hearing aid (in the ear)

heart

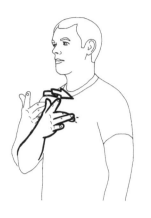

heart
Valentine

heart attack

heartbeat

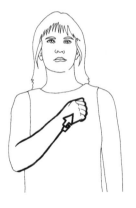

heartbeat

heaven

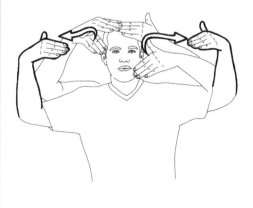

heavy

height (of an object)

height (of a person)

helicopter

hell

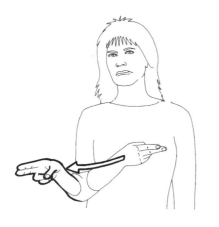

hello
hi
wave hello

helmet

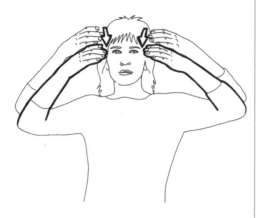

help
aid

help you

her (possessive)
his
its

here
present

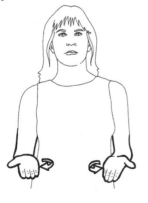

here

hers (possessive plural)
his

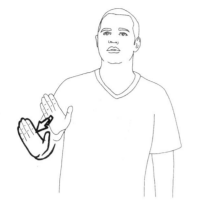

hide
conceal

high
altitude

high
hallucination

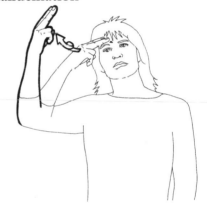

high heels

high heels
pumps

high heels
spikes

highway

hiking

hill

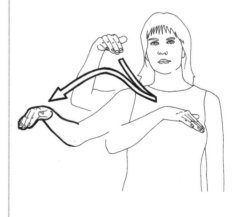

himself
herself
itself

hire

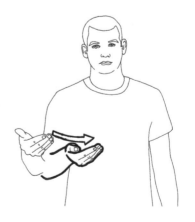

history

hit
beat
impact
strike

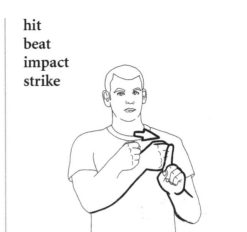

hockey

hold

hole
gap

Holland

Holland

holy
righteous

home

home run (#HR)

homework

Honduras
Houston

honest
truth
truthful

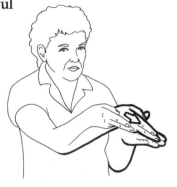

honey (person)

honey (food)

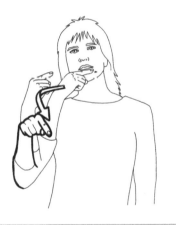

Hong Kong

honk horn

honor

hope
anticipate
expect

horse

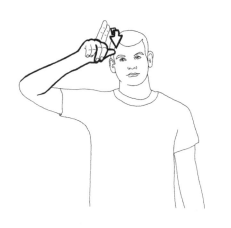

horseback riding

hospital
infirmary

hot
heat

hot dog

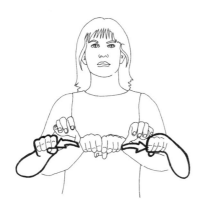

hotel

hour

house

how (how one is doing)

how (how to do something)

how many?

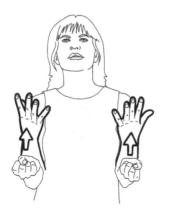

how much?

how much?

how much does it cost?

hug

huh?

humble
humility
meek

humble
humility
meek

hundred

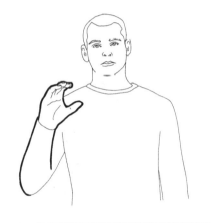

Hungary (ASL)

Hungary (Hungarian)

hungry
craving
hunger
starving

hunting

hurricane

hurricane

hurry
hurry up

hurt
ache
agony
harm
injury
pain
painful
sore
soreness

hurt (feelings)

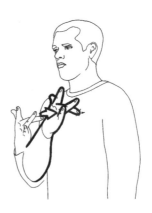

husband

hypocrite

I
me

ice cream
lollipop
sucker

Iceland

ice skating
skating

idea

identification

identify
identity

idiom
quotation
quote
subject
theme
title
topic

if
judge (verb)

if
suppose (formal)
imagine

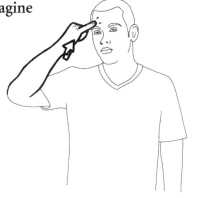

if (#IF)

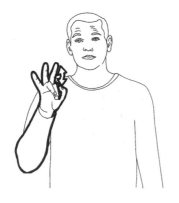

ignore

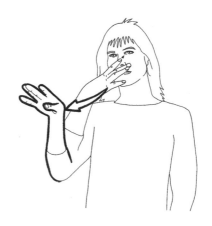

I love you

I love you

imagination

immature

important
counts
crucial
key
significant
valuable
worth

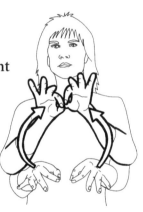

impossible

impressed

impressed with work

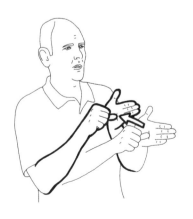

improve
doing better
gain
gradual
  improvement

improve
doing better
gain
significant
  improvement

in

include

increase
gain
raise

independent
independence

India

individual

Indonesia

industry

inferior

inflate

influence

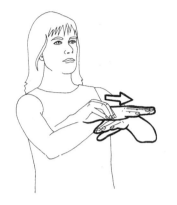

inform
information
let know
news
notify
report

inform everyone
inform all

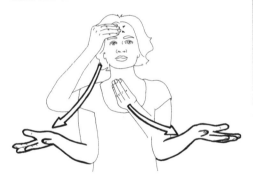

inform me

injection
give shot
shot
vaccination

injection
give shot
shot
vaccination

injection
give shot
shot
vaccination

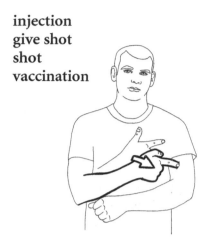

innocent
naïve

inside
indoors
stuffing

inspired

insult (verb)
put down (verb)

insurance
infection

intend
mean
purpose

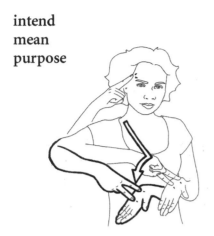

intercourse
sex

interest (money)

interest

interest

international (noun)

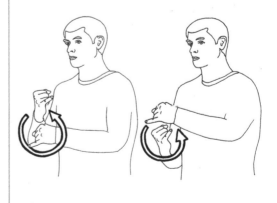

international (adjective)

Internet

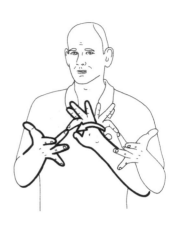

interpret

interpreter

 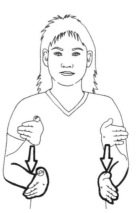

interrupt

interview

introduce
present
welcome

invent
create
fictionalize
make believe
make up

investigate

involve
take part in

Iran

Ireland (ASL)

Ireland (Irish)

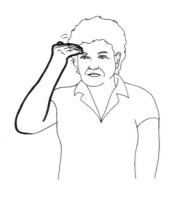

iron (noun)

iron (verb)

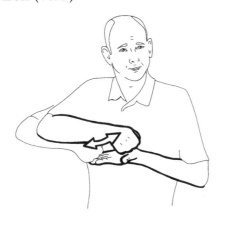

island

isolated

Israel (ASL)

Israel (Israeli)
Jewish

Istanbul

Italy (ASL)
Italian

Italy (Italian)
Italian

jail

Jamaica

Japan

jaw
jawbone

jealous
envious

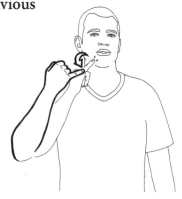

jelly
jam

jellyfish

Jerusalem

Jesus

jewelry

jigsaw puzzle
puzzle

job
work

job (#JOB)

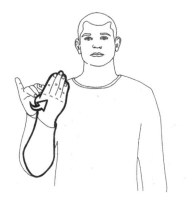

jogging

join
participate

Jordan

joy

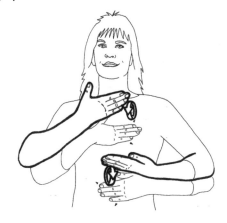

judge (noun)

jump

jump
leap

jump rope

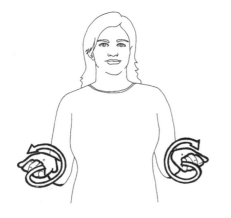

jump to conclusion

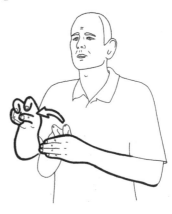

junior

junior

junior

kangaroo

Kansas City (K-C)

karate

keep

Kenya

ketchup
catsup

ketchup
catsup

ketchup
catsup

ketchup
catsup

key

kick

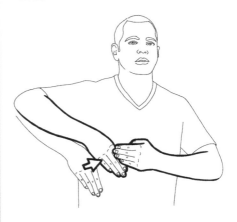

kid

kill
murder
slay

kind
type

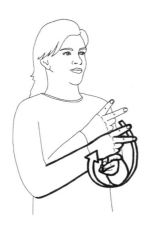

kindergarten
kitchen

king

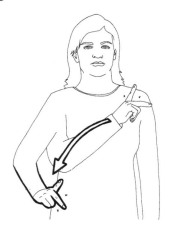

kingdom

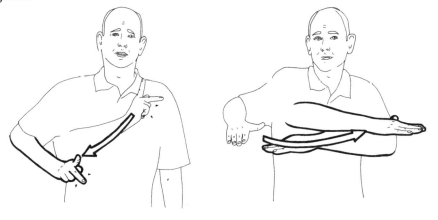

kiss

kite (noun)

knee

kneel

knife

knife

knock
rap

know
aware
conscious
familiar
knowledge

know that

Korea

Kuwait

ladder

ladder

lady
woman

lady
woman

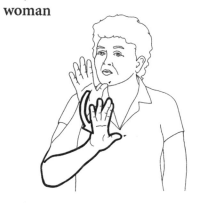

laid up

lake
pond

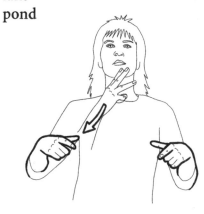

lamb

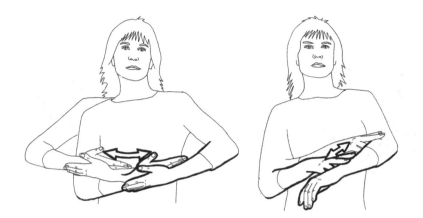

land
area
field
property

language
dialect
tongue

lantern

lap

laptop computer

large

last
final
lastly

last night

last week

last year

late
tardy
not yet
yet

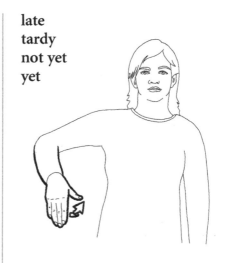

later
after awhile

laugh

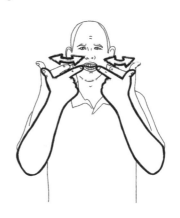

law
legal

lawn sprinkler
sprinkler

lawyer
attorney

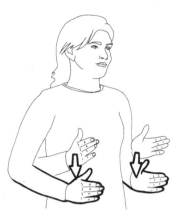

lay off

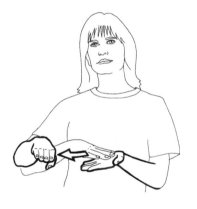

lazy

leaf
feather

learn

leather

leather

leave
depart
go away
go out

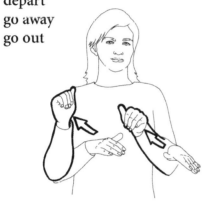

Lebanon

lecture
address
presentation
sermon
speech
talk

left (direction)

left arm

leg

legislature

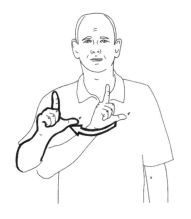

lemon

lend
loan

lesbian

lesson

let
allow

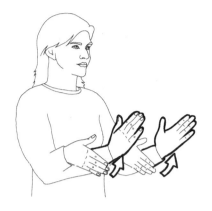

letter
mail

lettuce
cabbage

level
even

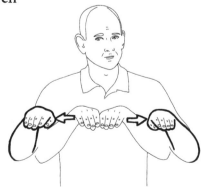

liar

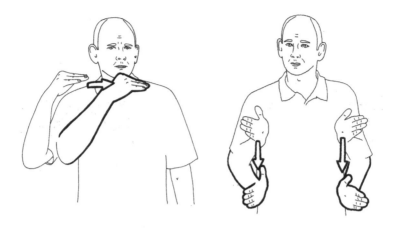

liar

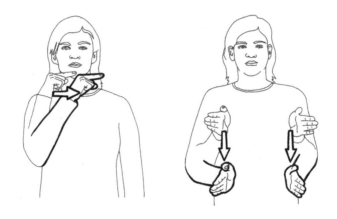

librarian

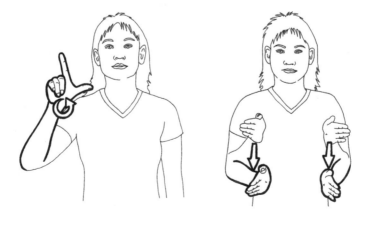

library

license
permit

lick

lie (noun and verb)
falsehood
fib

lie (verb)

life
live

lift

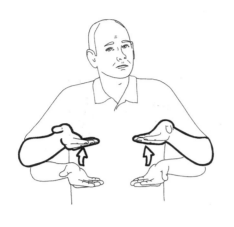

light
lightbulb

lighthouse

lighthouse

lightning

lights off
lights out

lights on

light (weight)
lightweight

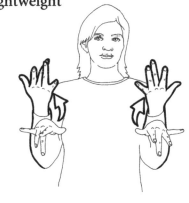

like

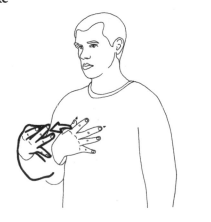

limit
restrict

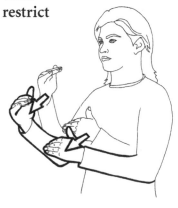

line
straight line

line (on a page)

line up

lion

lipreading

lips

lipstick

list

listen
hear

little
small
tiny

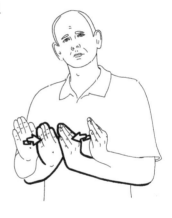

live
alive
dwell
life
survive

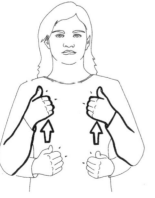

living room

living room

loaf (of bread)

 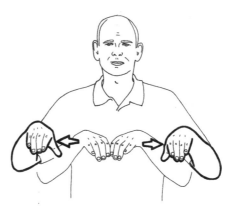

loaf (verb)
laze

lobster
crabs

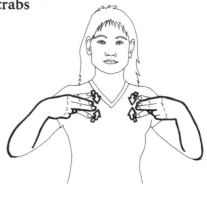

lock up
lock

London

lonely
lonesome

long (measure)
length

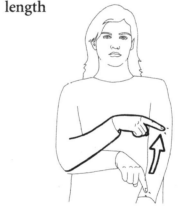

long ago

look

look
browse

look at
watch

look at me

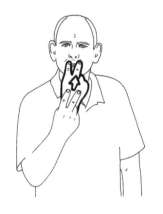

look back
memory

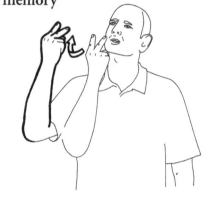

look down

look forward

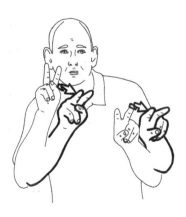

look like
resemble

look like
resemble

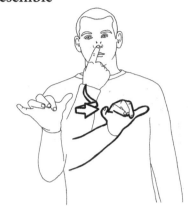

looks (noun)

looks familiar

look up (verb)

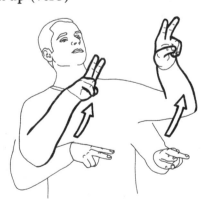

loose

Lord

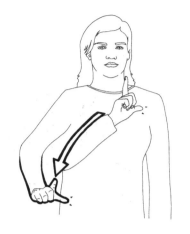

Lord

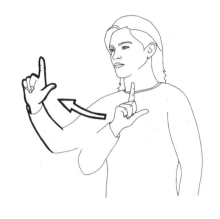

Los Angeles (L-A)

lose (competition)

lose (object)
loss
lost

lose weight

loud

loudspeaker

loudspeaker

lousy

love

lover

 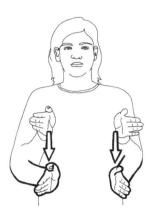

low
cut back
decrease
less
lessen

low

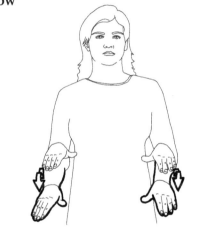

lower-case letter

lucky

lunch

lunch

lungs

Lutheran

 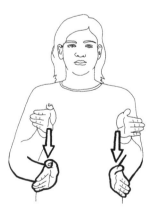

machine
engine
factory
mechanism
plant

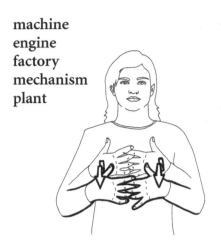

machine running

magazine
brochure
catalog
pamphlet

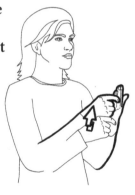

magic

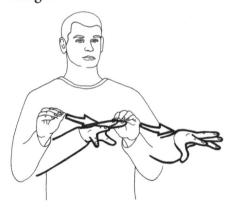

magnet

main
major

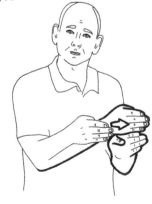

mainstream (verb)
integrate

make
manufacture
produce

makeup brush

makeup powder

Malaysia

male haircut

man (can also be signed with a 5
   handshape in both positions)
guy
male

man
guy
male

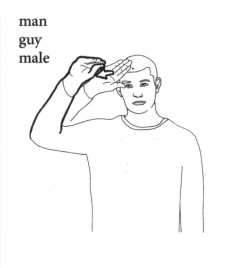

manager
director

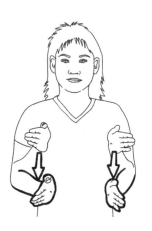

manhole

many
lots
numerous

march

marijuana
pot

marriage

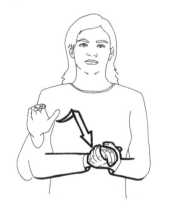

marry

mask

mask

match
fit
mate

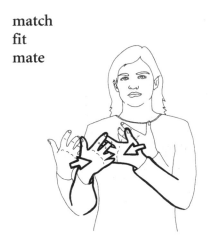

material
object

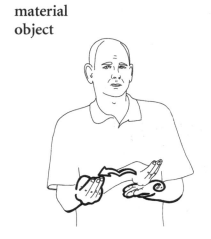

material
cloth
fabric

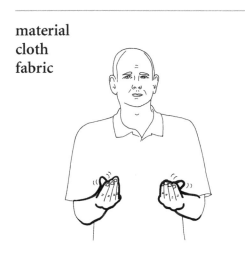

mathematics
math

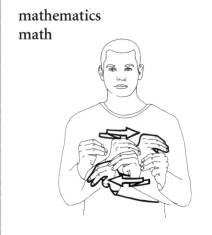

mattress

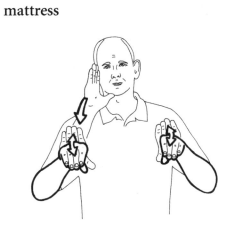

maybe
might
perhaps
probably

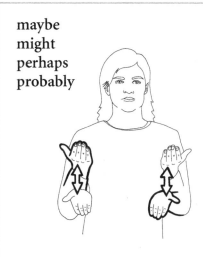

mayonnaise (M-A-Y-O)

mean
cruel
harsh
rude
unkind

measles

measure
inches
miles
size

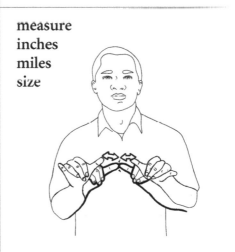

meat
beef
content
flesh
steak
substance

mediate

medicine
poison

meditate

meditation

medium

meet (verb)

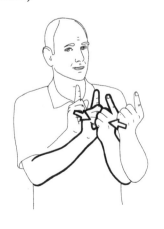

meeting
convention
session

member

memorize

menstruation
period

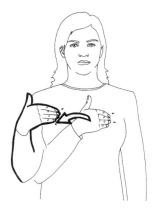

mentally retarded (#MR)

mention

merry-go-round
carnival
fair

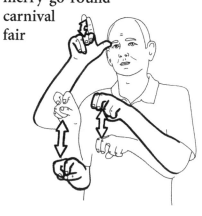

merry-go-round
carnival
fair

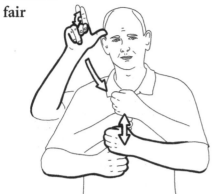

mesh
blend

mess
messy

message

messenger
courier

metal
steel

method

Methodist

 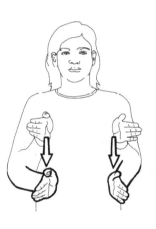

me too
I agree with you
same

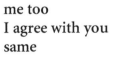

Mexico

Mexico

Mexico
Mormons

Miami

microphone

microwave

microwave (#MW)

midnight

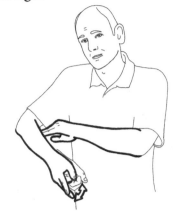

midnight

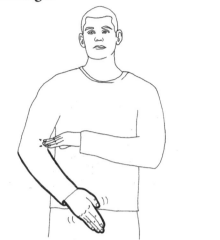

Milan

milk

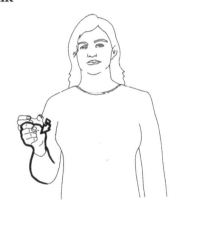

milk a cow

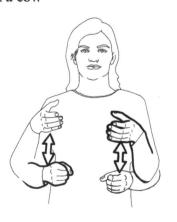

milkshake
shake

million

millionaire

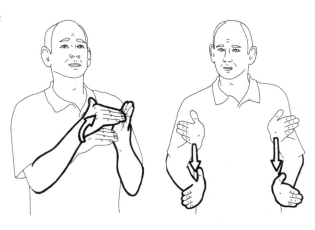

Milwaukee

mine (adjective)

minimum

Minneapolis

minor

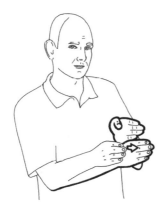

minor
under age

minor
insignificant
nothing to it

minute
moment

mirror

mischievous
naughty

mischievous
naughty

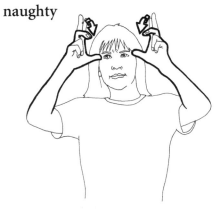

miscommunication

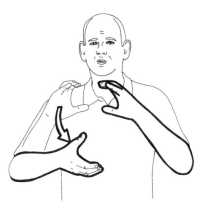

miscommunication
misunderstanding

miss (to miss a person)

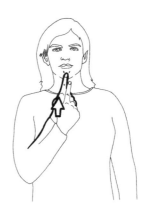

miss
skip an event

mission

missionary

mistake
error

misunderstand

mix
scramble

model

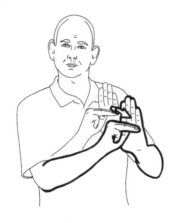

mold (verb)
shape

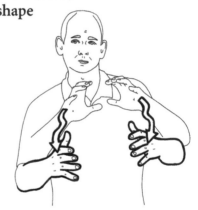

Monday

money
funds

monkey
ape
chimpanzee
gorilla

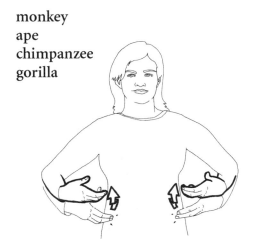

Montana

month

monthly
rent

moon

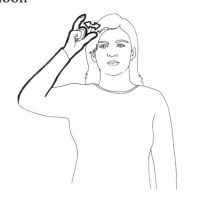

mop

mother-in-law

motion
movement

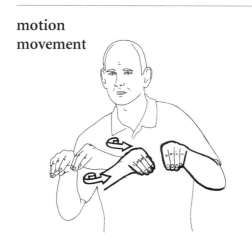

motor
car motor

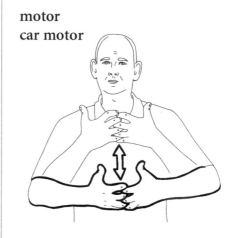

motor

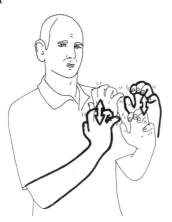

motorcycle
moped
snowmobile

mountain

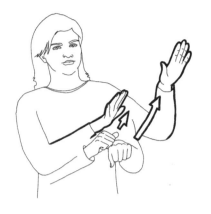

mouse

mouth

move

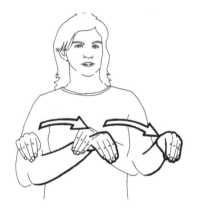

move away

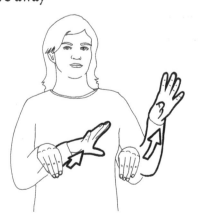

movie
cinema
film

movie
cinema
film

movie screen

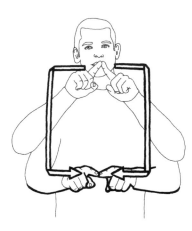

mow

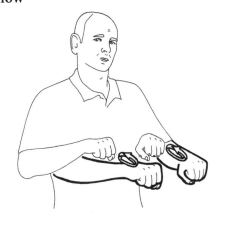

mull over
think about

mumps

museum

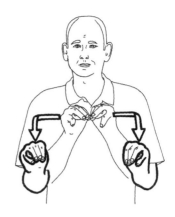

music

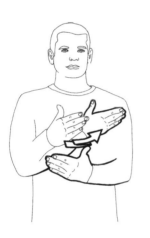

Muslim

must
should

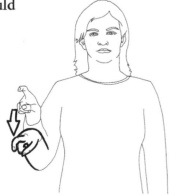

mustache

my
mine

my fault

myself

myself

nab
get a hold of

naked
nude

name

Namibia

napkin

napkin

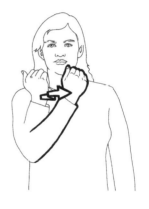

narrow
focus

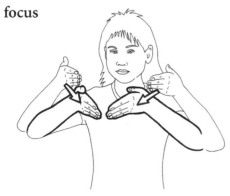

narrow

narrow column

narrow-minded

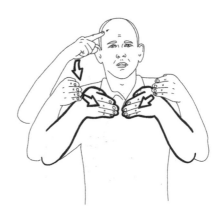

nation
national

Native American
American Indian

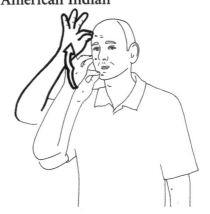

Native American
American Indian

natural
naturally
nature

nauseous

navy (military)

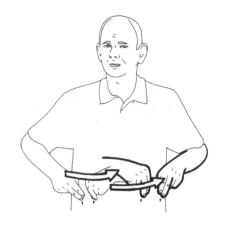

near
nearby

neat
cool

neck

necklace

need
have to
necessary
needs
need to
ought to
supposed to

negative

neighbor

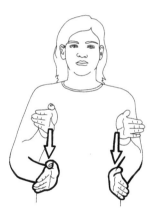

neighborhood

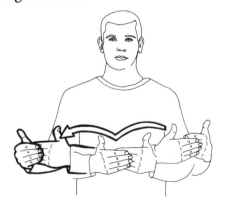

neither

nephew

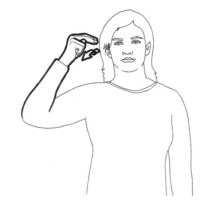

nerve

nerve
nervy

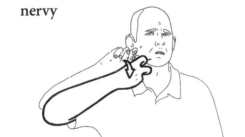

nervous
apprehensive

net

neutral

never

new
fresh

New Orleans

newspaper

New Testament

New York

New Zealand

next
adjacent
by

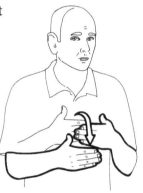

next week

next year

nibble

noisy
noise

none
nothing

none
nothing

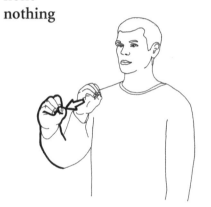

noon
twelve o'clock

north

North America

Norway

nose

not

not funny (serious)
come on

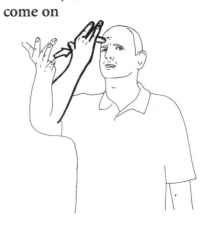

not funny (teasing)
come on

nothing
none

nothing changes
same old thing
same-same
tedious

notice
acknowledge
recognize

not interested

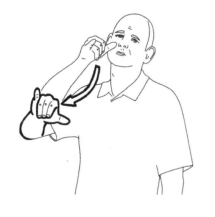

not interested

not yet
not yet done
unfinished

now

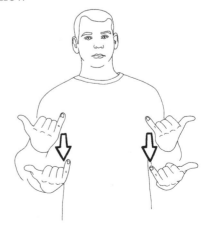

now

number

nun

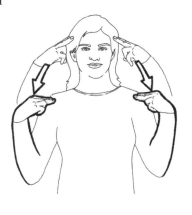

nurse

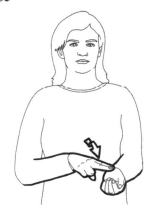

obey

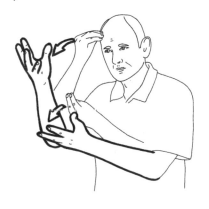

ocean

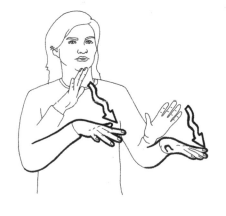

octopus

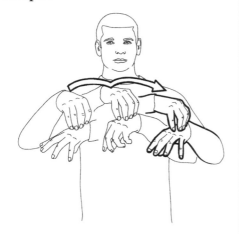

of course

off

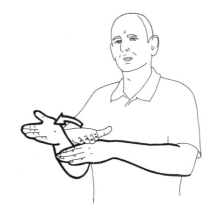

#OFF

offer
move (parliamentary procedure)
propose
recommend
suggest

office

often
frequent
frequently

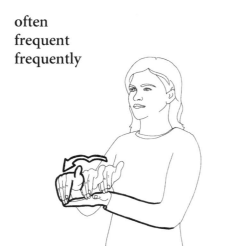

oh I see
I understand
we'll see

oh I see
I understand
we'll see

okay (#OK)

old

one-half

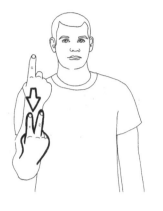

one hundred

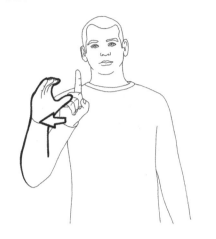

one million

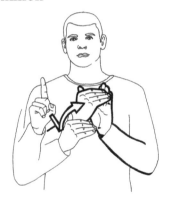

one more

one more

one-third

one-third

one thousand

onion

Ontario

open

open book (verb)

oral

oral

orange

organ (musical instrument only)

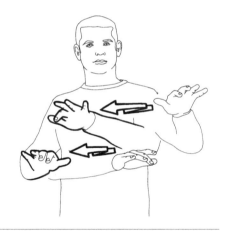

organization

orthodox

Orthodox (Jewish)

---

other
else

our
ours

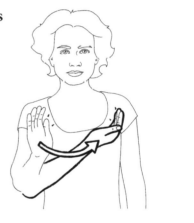

---

ourselves

out

outline

outside
outdoors

overdo (verb)

overflow
run over

overhead projector

owl

pack

page (in book)

pager (voice/vibrating
alerting device)

pager (text alerting device,
more often used by
deaf people)

paint

paintbrush

painter

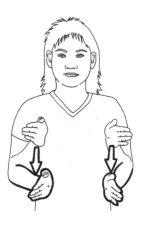

pajamas

Pakistan

pale
wan

Palestine

Panama

pancake

pants
jeans
slacks
trousers

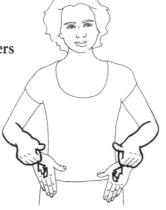

paper

paper clip
clip

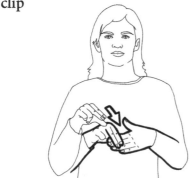

parade
procession

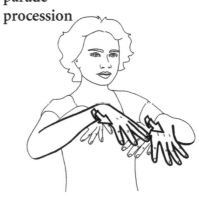

paragraph

Paraguay

parallel

paranoid
insane

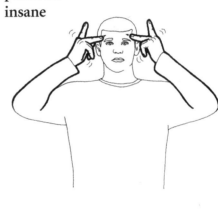

paranoid
insane

parents

Paris

park (verb)
parking

parking meter

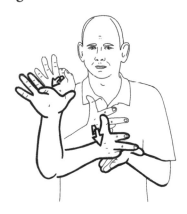

Parliament

participate

participate

partner (business)

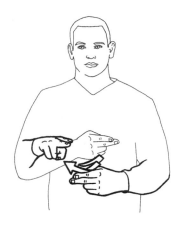

party

pass by
go ahead of

password
confidential
personal
private
secret

past
ago
a while ago
back
before
previous
previously
was
were

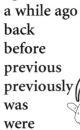

pat

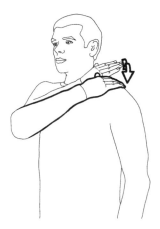

patch

patient (noun)

patient
bear
patience
put up with
stand
take
tolerate

pay
payment

pay
payment

pay attention

peace
calm
peaceful
serene

peach (same sign for fruit and color)

peak
mountain top
tip

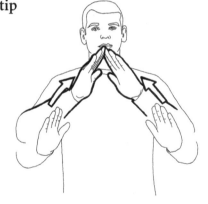

peanuts
nuts

pear

peel paint • 329

pearls

peas

peek

peel a banana

peel an orange (or other thick substance)

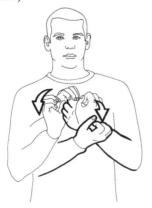

peel paint (or other thin substance)

peel skin

peel with a knife

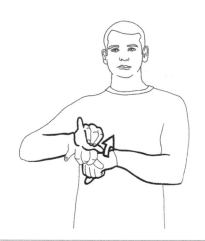

pen

pencil

penguin

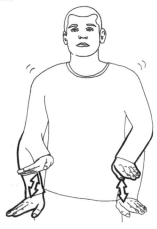

penis (formal)

penis (informal)

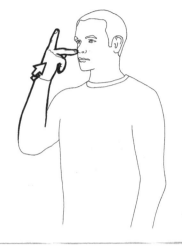

people

pepper

pepperoni pizza

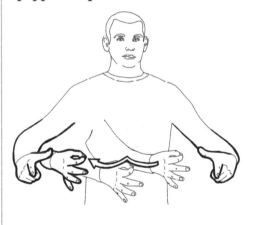

percent
percentage

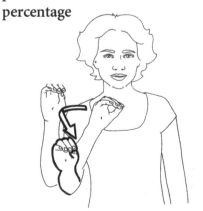

perfect
exact
perfection

perfect

perfect fit

perfume

perfume

period
decimal point
dot
point

period
point on page

permit (verb)

person

personality

person lying
down

person rolling

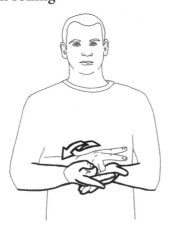

person running
running

perspective

perspective

persuade
urge

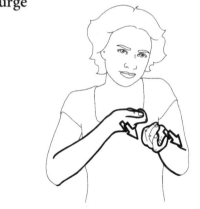

Peru

Peru

pet (verb)

pet (noun)
spoiled person

Philadelphia

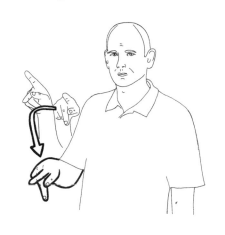

Philippine Islands

Philippine Islands

philosophy

Phoenix

photograph
image
picture

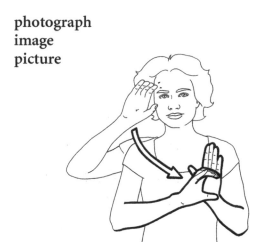

---

photographer

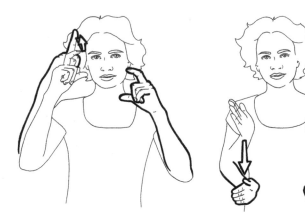

---

physical

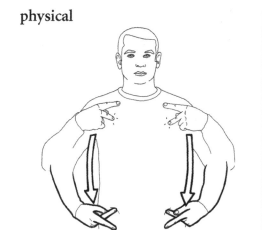

physical education (P-E)

physics

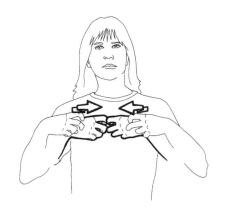

piano

pickle

picnic

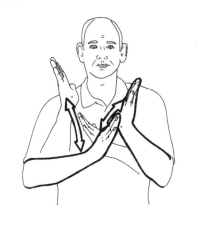

pie

pig
hog
pork

pile (verb)
stack

pile (noun)
stack

pile
heap of clothes

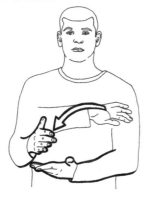

pillow

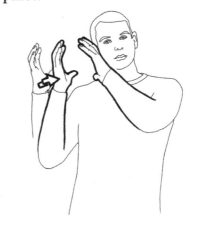

pillow
cushion

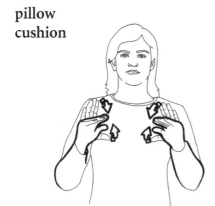

pills (noun)
tablets

pilot

pimples

pimples

pin

pin
badge

pinball

pineapple

ping pong
table tennis

ping pong
table tennis

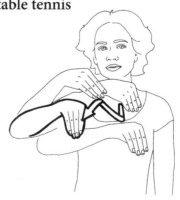

pink

pipe (wide)
tube

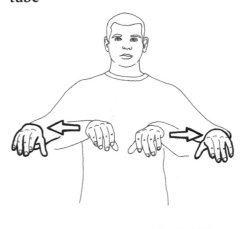

pipe (smoking)

pitch
vocal range

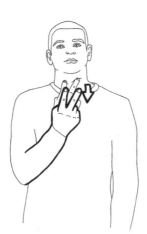
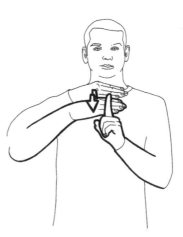

pitch (a ball)

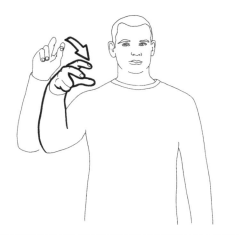

pitcher

pitcher

Pittsburgh
Maine

pity
compassion
mercy
poor baby
sympathy

pizza

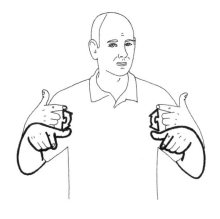

pizza

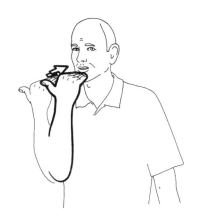

pizza

pizza (#PIZZA)

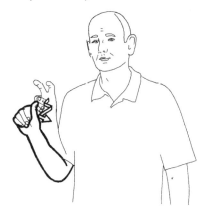

place
location
position
site

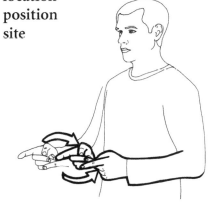

plain

plan
organize

plant (verb)

play
party
recess

player

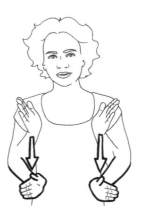

playful

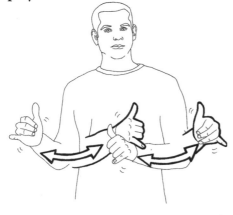

playground

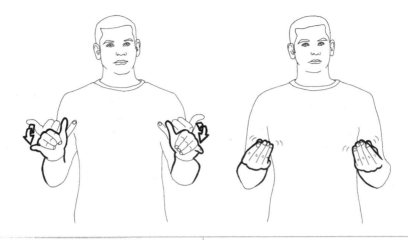

pleasant (weather)
cool

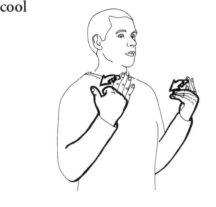

please

plenty
ample

plug (verb)

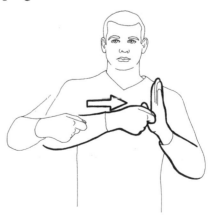

plug (noun)

plumber

pneumonia

pneumonia

pocket

poem (ASL)

poem (English)

point (gesturing motion)

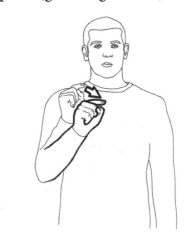

pointing (to a place)

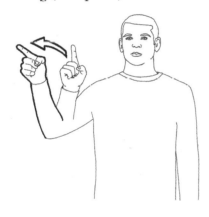

poke

Poland

Poland

pole (thin)
stick
thin pipe

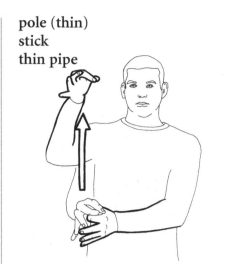

police
cop
officer
sheriff

policy
principle

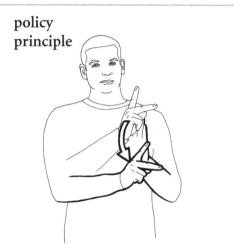

polite
courteous
well behaved
well mannered

politics
political

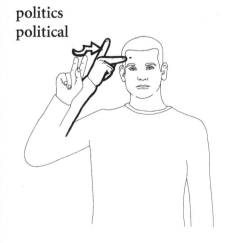

pool
billiards

poor
destitute
impoverished

pop a cork

popcorn

Portugal

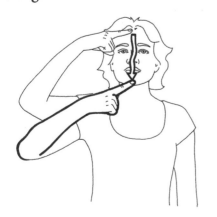

positive
plus

possible
able
capable
possibly

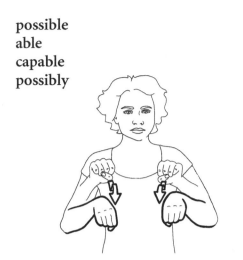

poster
bulletin board
notice
sign

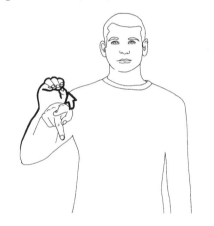

poster
bulletin board
notice
sign

post office (P-O)

postpone
delay
put off

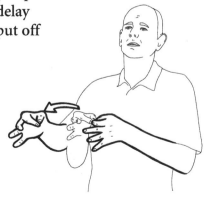

potato

pour

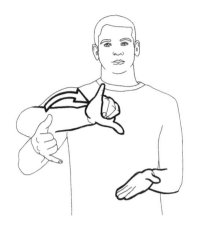

pour

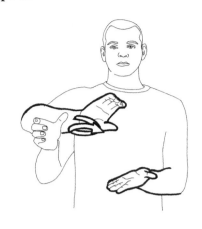

power

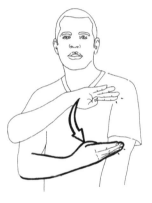

powerful

practice
drill
exercise
rehearse

praise
clap hands

pray
prayer

preach

preacher
minister
pastor
reverend

predict
forecast
foresee
foretell
Mohammed
prophesize

prefer
favorite
preference
want

prefer
preference
rather

pregnant

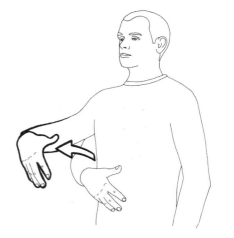

pregnant

prepare

Presbyterian

preschool

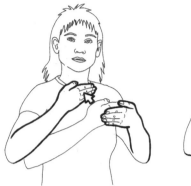 

preschool

president
superintendent

pressure
stress

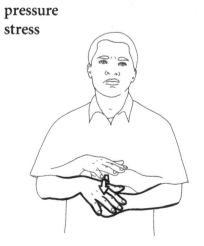

pretend
create

pretty
beautiful
lovely

prevent
bar
barrier
block
guard
obstruct
prevention
protect

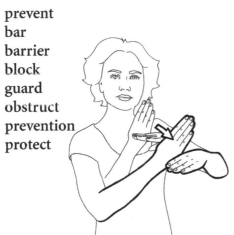

priest

primary

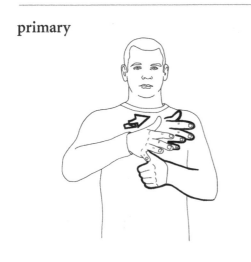

prince

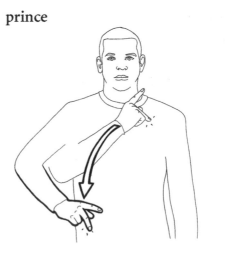

princess

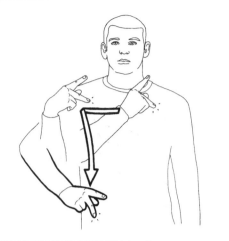

principal

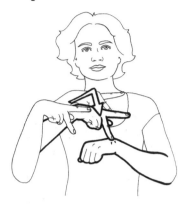

print
press
publish

printer

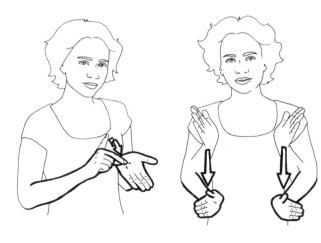

priority

prison

prisoner

privilege

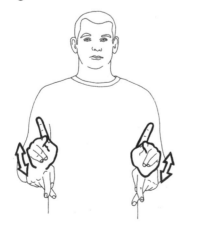

problem
difficulty

problem
difficulty

problem
difficulty

process

procrastinate

profession
area
field
line of work

program

progress
progressive

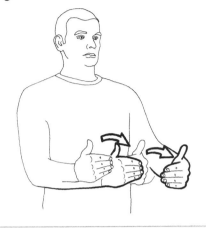

project

promise
commit
dedicate
obligate
obligation
pledge

promote
advance
progress
promotion

proof
evidence

psychologist

psychology

puddle

Puerto Rico

Puerto Rico

pull (verb)
draw

pumpkin

punch (verb)

punch (verb)

punish
condemn
penalize

puppet

purple

purse
handbag
pocketbook

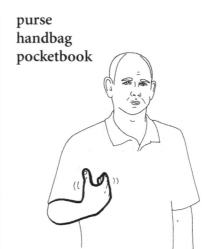

push
shove

put
place

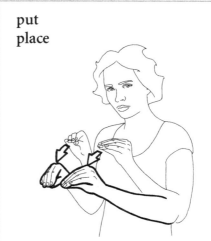

put in

put in one's place
bring down to size
humble someone

put on blanket

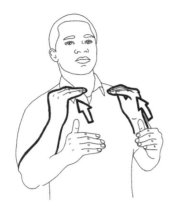

put on hearing aid

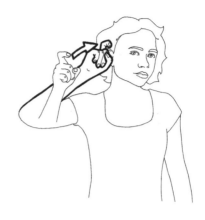

put on ring

puzzled
perplexed
stymied

Quaker

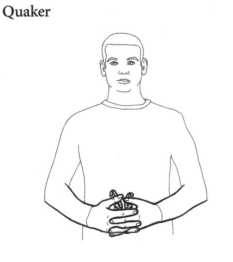

quarrel
argument
controversy
debate
dispute

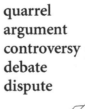
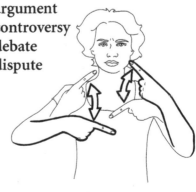

quarter
twenty-five cents

Quebec

queen

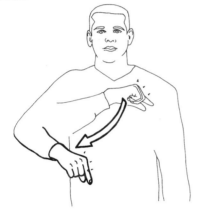

question

quiet
peaceful
silence
silent
still

quit
drop out

rabbi

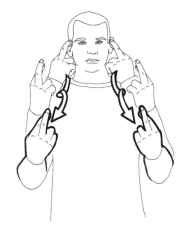

rabbi

rabbit
bunny

raccoon

radio

rain

rainbow

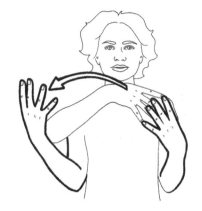

raindrops

rain sprinkles

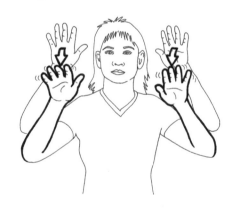

rake (verb)
raking

ram

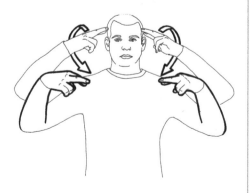

ram

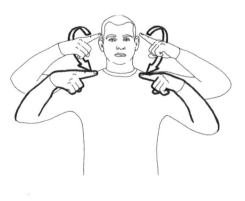

range (age)

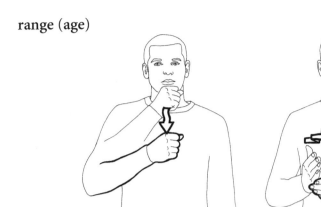

range (land)
acreage

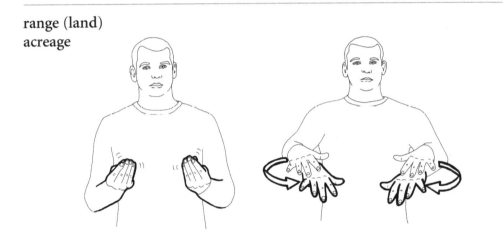

raspberry

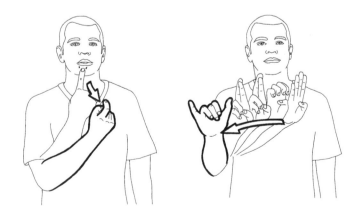

rat

rattlesnake

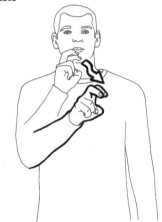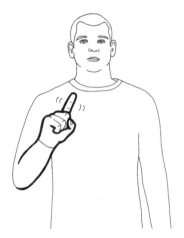

read

reading

ready

reason
rationale
realize

recently
a little bit ago
a short
    time ago
just

recline

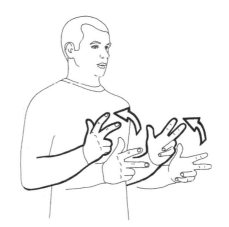

recommend

record (noun)
LP

recover

red

reduce
lose weight
slim down

reduce
cut down
decrease
make smaller

refer

refer

reflect

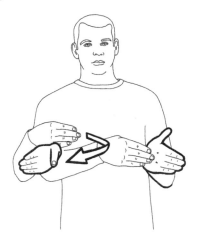

refrigerator

refrigerator (R-E-F)

refuse
decline
won't

register
sign in
sign up

register
sign in
sign up

regular
ordinary
proper
usual

rehabilitation (R-E-H-A-B)

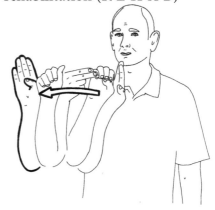

reinforce
support

reinforce
support

reins

reject

relationship
association

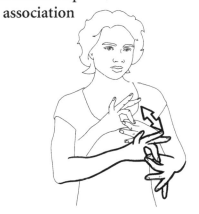

relationship off
break ott
break up
relationship
  over

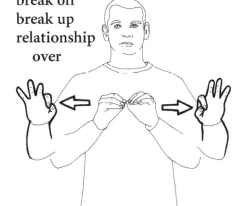

relative

relative

relax
relaxed
rest

release
let go

release
let go

relief
relieved

religion
religious

remain
stay

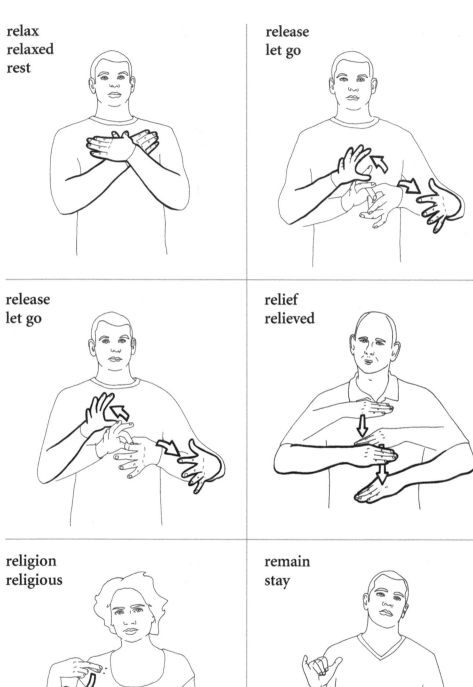

remember
recall
recollect

remind

remind

remind another person

remind me

remove
deduct

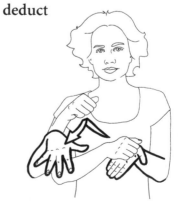

remove
delete
discard

repair

report

report

reporter
newscaster

reporter
journalist

represent

represent

representative

representative

Republican

research

research

researcher

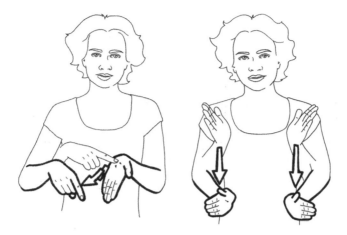

researcher

reserve
reservation

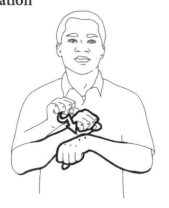

residential school
institute
institution
school for
the deaf

resign

respect
look up to

responsibility
burden
charge
responsible

responsibility
burden
charge
responsible

restaurant

restless
antsy

restless
antsy

restroom

result
consequence
outcome

result
consequence
outcome

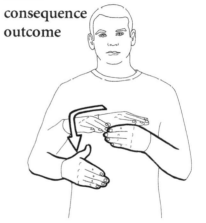

resurrection

resurrection

retire
end career

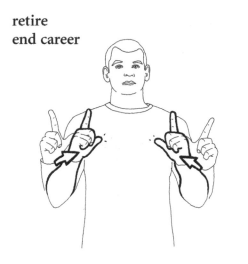

retire
end career

retire

revenge
get back at
get even with

review

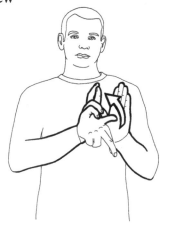

revival

rib

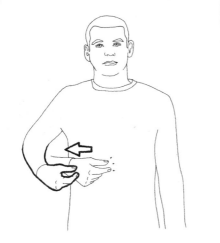

ribbon

ribs

rich
prosperous
wealth
wealthy

rich
prosperous
wealth
wealthy

Richmond
Rochester, New York

ride (vehicle)

ride (on an animal—repeated
movement)

ride (on an animal—single
movement)

ridiculous
absurd

rifle

rifle
shotgun

right
correct

right (direction)

right (legal)

right arm

ring (noun)

rip
tear

rip-off (verb)

rise
bread rising

river

river

road
avenue
lane
method
path
street
trail
way

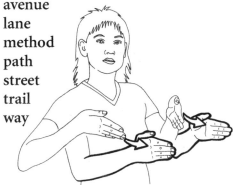

rock (noun)
stone

rocket
missile
space shuttle

rocking chair

rollerblading

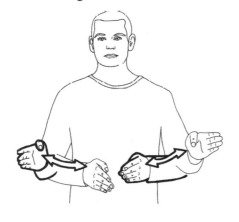

rollerskating
skating

Rome

roof

room

roommate

rooster
cock

roots

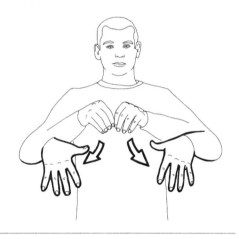

rope

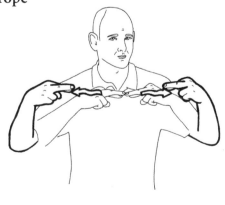

rose

Rosh Hoshanah
Happy New Year

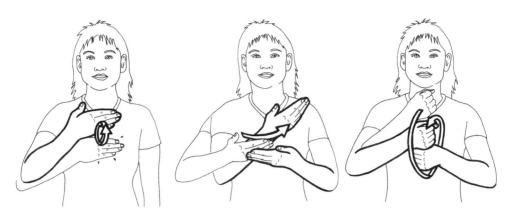

rough
coarse
crude

royal

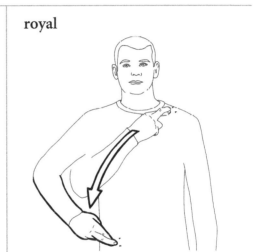

royal

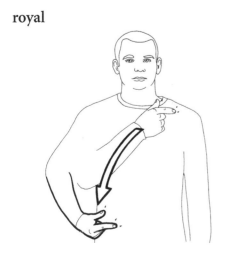

rub
scrub

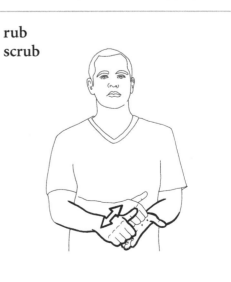

rubber

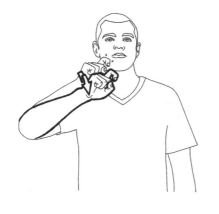

rugged (texture)

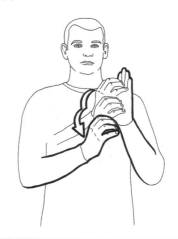

ruin
spoil

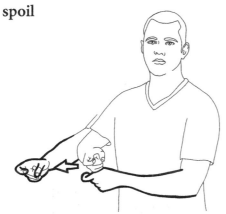

rule
principle
regulation

run
in a hurry

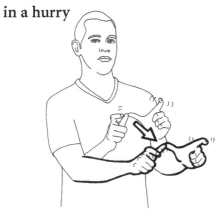

run (in hose)

running water
leak

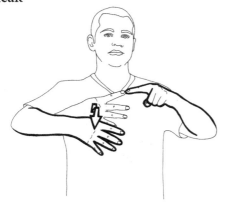

runny nose

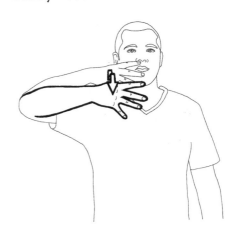

Russia (Russian)

Russia (ASL)
Newfoundland

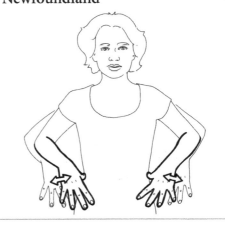

sad
mournful
tragic
unhappy

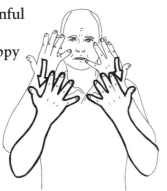

sailboat (noun)

sailing (verb)
boating

St. Louis

St. Paul

salad

sales pitch

salt

same
alike
also
in common
like
mutual
similar

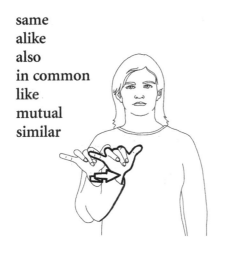

same
alike
also
in common
like
mutual
similar

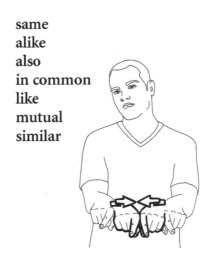

same time
simultaneously

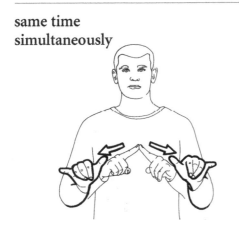

San Antonio

sandals
flip flops

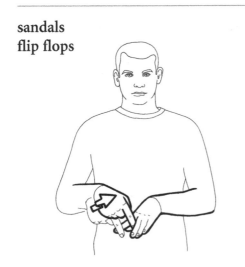

San Diego (S-D)

sandwich
picnic

San Francisco (S-F)

Santa Claus

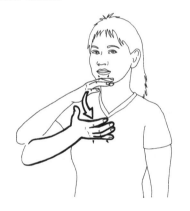

satisfied
contented
satisfaction

Saturday

sauce
salad dressing
syrup

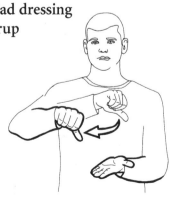

Saudi Arabia

save
free
liberate
redeem
rescue
safe
salvation
secure

save
keep
preserve

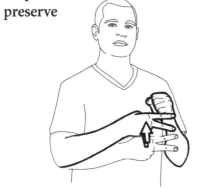

save money

Savior

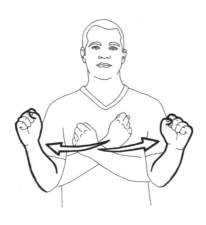

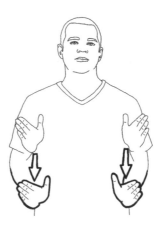

saw (noun)

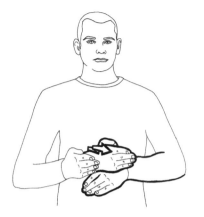

say

scale
pound
weight

Scandinavia

scared

scarf

school

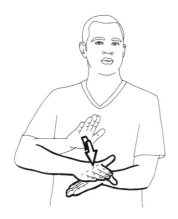

science

scientist

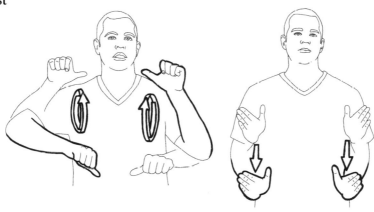

scissors
clippers

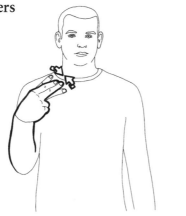

scissors
shears

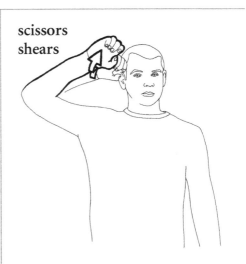

scold
reprimand

scooter

Scotland (Scottish)

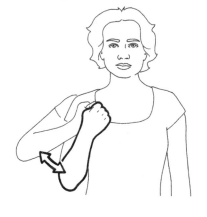

scout

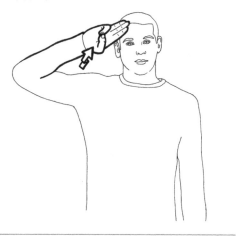

scrape

screen (verb)

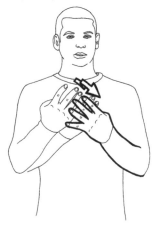

screwdriver

scrounge

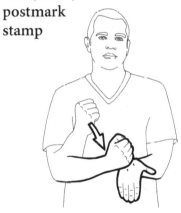

scuba diving

seal (noun)
postmark
stamp

search
look for

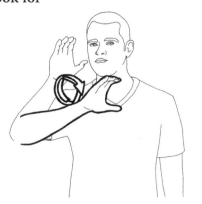

second (ordinal number)

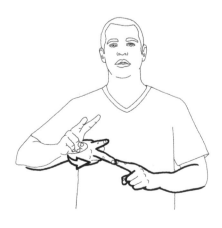

second (time unit)

secretary

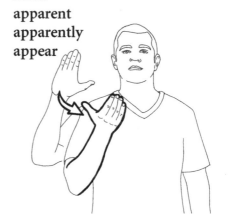

see
eyesight
sight
vision

seem
apparent
apparently
appear

seesaw

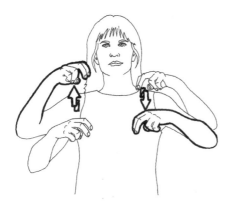

self

selfish
greedy

sell

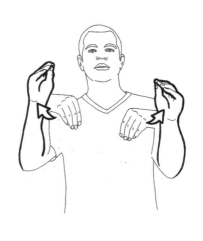

senate

senator

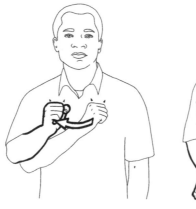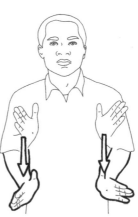

send

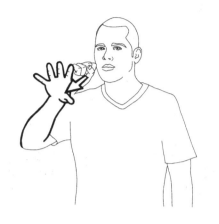

send
mail

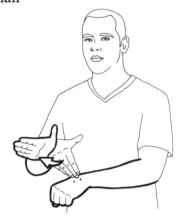

send a telegram

send a telegram

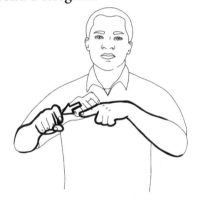

senior

senior citizen

sensitive

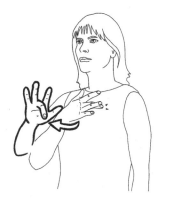

sentence
statement

separate
apart
part
separated

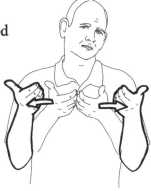

servant

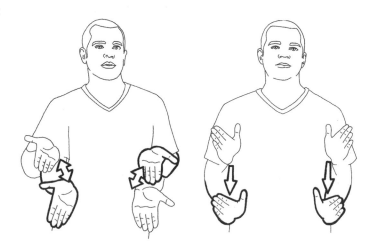

serve
minister (verb)
service
wait on

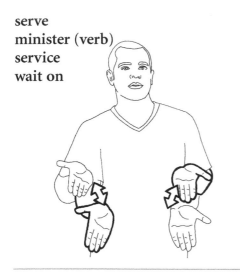

set up (verb)
erect

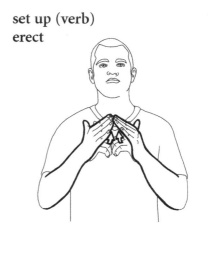

set up (verb)

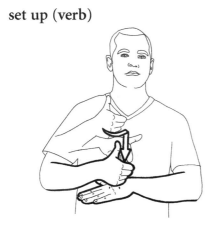

seven

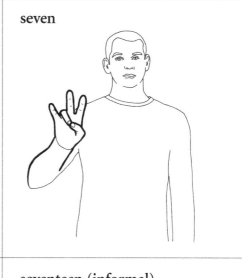

seventeen (formal)

seventeen (informal)

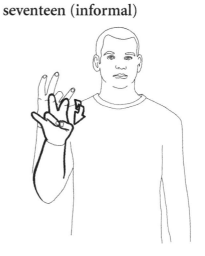

several
few

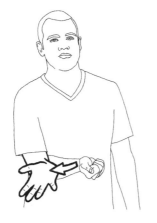

sew

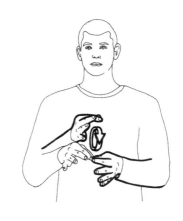

sew
sewing

sewing machine

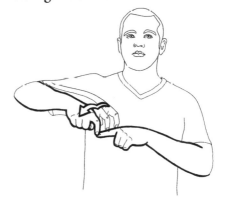

sex
gender

shade
dark

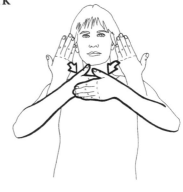

shadow

shake (verb)

shake
shaking a tree

shame

shampoo

Shanghai

sharp
pointed (object)

shave

shave

sheep

shelf
mantle

shiny
bright
glow
shine
shining

ship (noun)

shirt
top

shock
astonish
astound
dumbfound

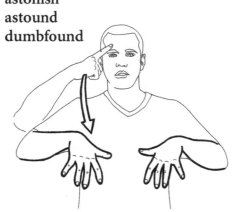

shock
astonish
astound
dumbfound

shoes

shoot
shot

shopping
shop

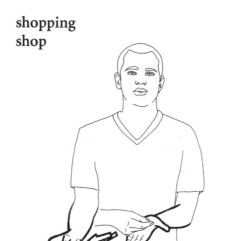

short
small

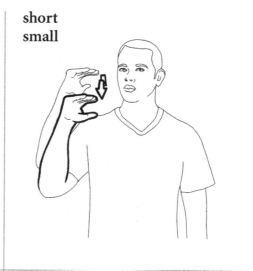

short (time)
brief

shorts

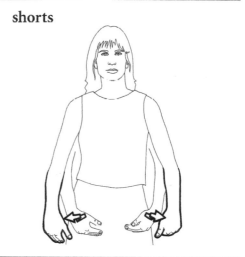

short sleeves

shot-up

shovel

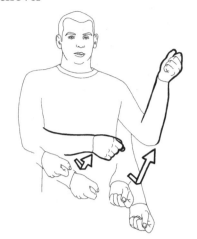

show
demonstrate
example
reveal
sample

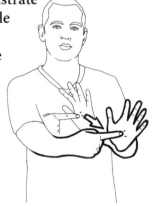

shower

shut up

shy
bashful

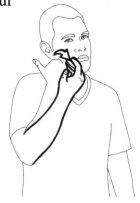

sick
disease
ill
illness
sickness

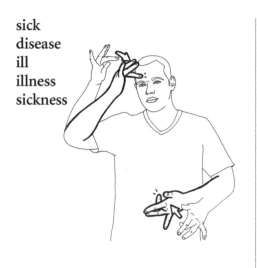

side

sign

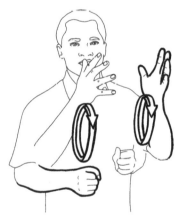

sign
billboard

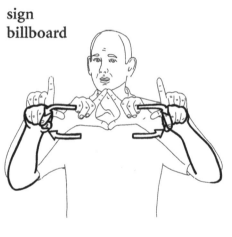

signature

sign language

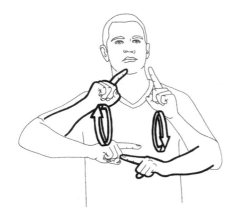

silly
foolish

silver
shiny

similar

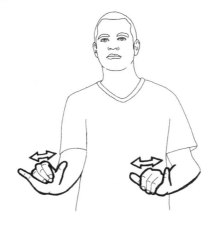

simple

sin

since
all along
ever since
have been
so far
up to now

sing
hymn
song

Singapore

singer

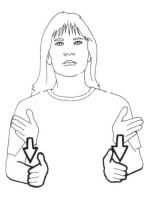

single
unmarried

single

single
swinging single

sinned

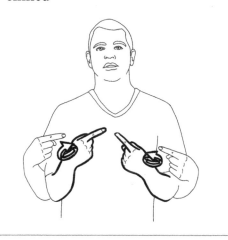

sister

sister

sister-in-law

sit
sit down

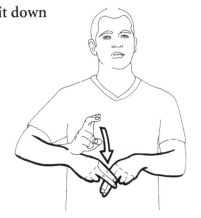

situation

six

sixteen (formal)

sixteen (informal)

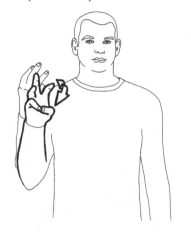

skateboard

skeleton
bones

skeptical
doubtful

skiing

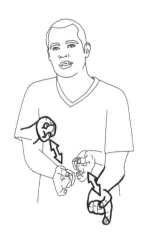

skin

skinny

skirt

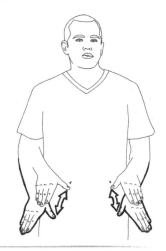

skunk

sky

skyscraper

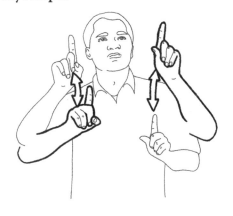

slave

sleep

sleep

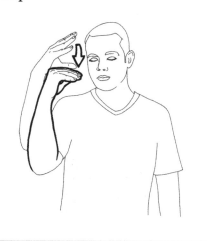

sleepy
drowsy

sleeves
shirt sleeves

slice (verb)
cut with knife

sliding doors

slip (verb)
slide

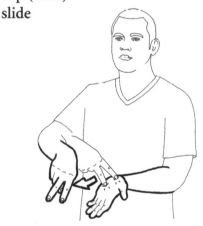

slippers

slippery (adj.)

slow
slowly

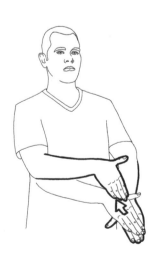

sly
adventurous
secretively
sneaky
stealthy

smart
bright
clever
intellect
intelligence
intelligent
sharp

smell
fragrance
odor
scent

smile
grin

smoke

smoking

smooth
fluent

smooth
fluent

smooth
(surface)

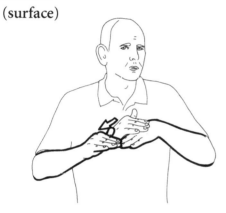

snake

sneeze

snorkeling

snow

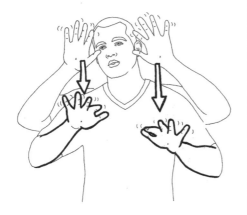

snowboarding

snowboarding

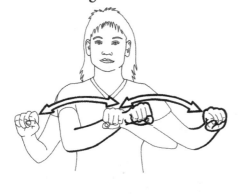

soap

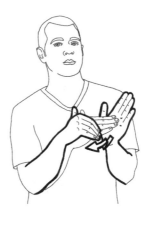

soccer

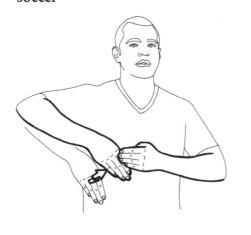

Social Studies (#SS)

social work (#SW)

social worker

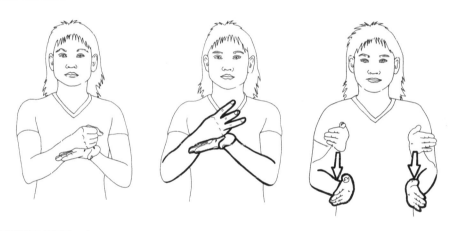

society

socks

sophisticated
sophistication

sophomore

sophomore

sophomore

sore throat

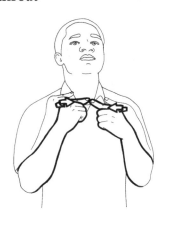

sorry
apologize
apology
pardon
regret

soul

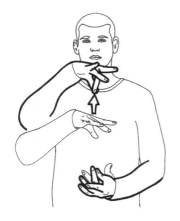

soup
spoon

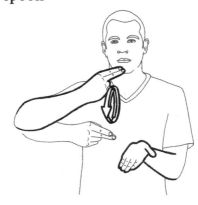

sour
bitter
lemon
tart

south
southern

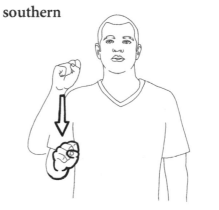

south
southern

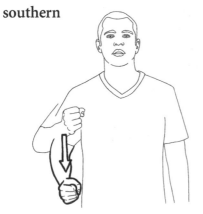

South Africa

South America

spaghetti

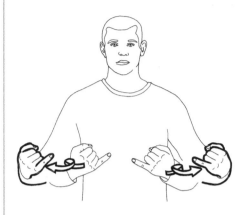

Spain

spank

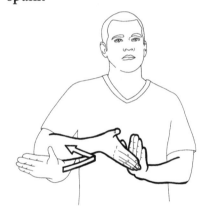

speak

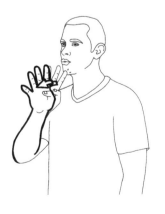

special
except
unique

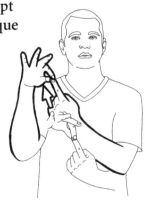

specialty
specialize

specific
point (of discussion)

speech
speechreading

speedometer

spend

spend

spend

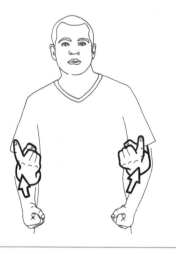

spicy

spicy

spicy

spider

spin

spit

sports
athletics
competition
contest
race

spring
plants

square

stand up (from sitting)

standard
same
uniform

stare

stare at each other

stars

start
begin
commence
originate

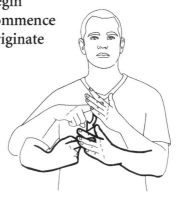

state

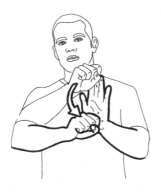

statue
shape

stay
remain

steal
rob

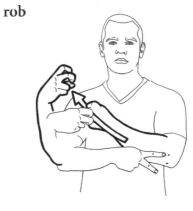

stealth
secretive
sneakily

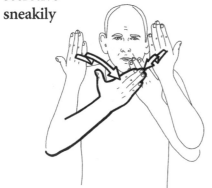

steam

steam

steep

steeple

stepbrother

stepfather

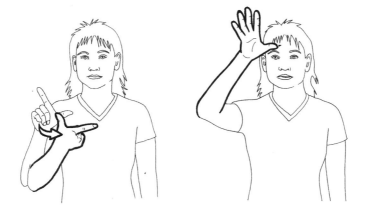

stepmother

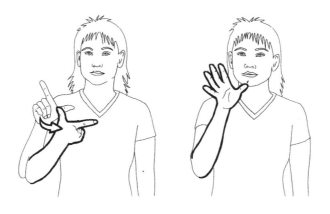

stepsister

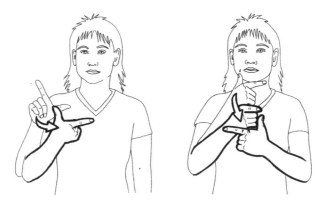

steps

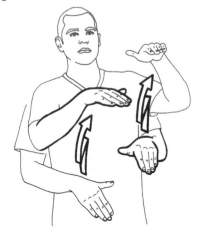

sticky

still (yet)

stimulate

sting

sting

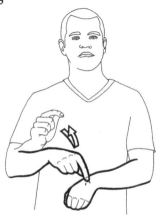

stingy
miserly

stingy

stink
smelly

stink
smelly

stir (verb)
whip

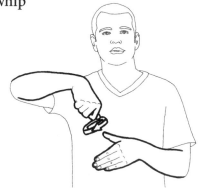

stockings
hose

straight

strange
odd
peculiar
weird

straw (for drinking)

strawberry

strawberry

stray (verb)
deviate
go off topic
wander

stretch

strict

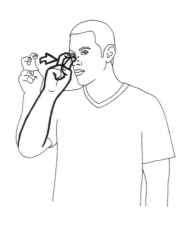

strike
protest
rebel
rebellion
revolt

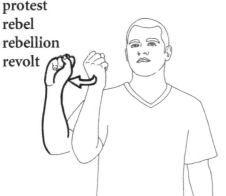

strike
bowling strike

strike a match
light a match

string

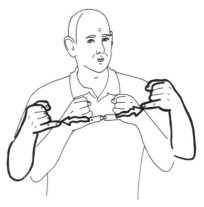

stripe

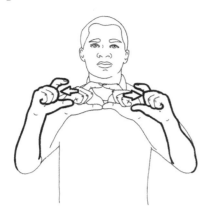

stripes (many)

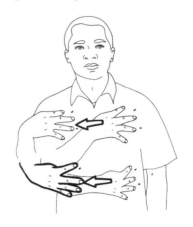

stripes (thin)

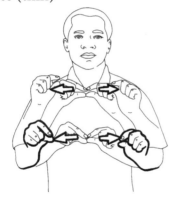

stripes (wide)

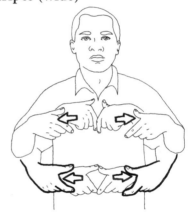

strip paint
remove paint

strong
brave
confidence
courageous
might
mighty
strength

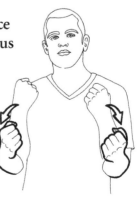

strong

structure

struggle

stubborn
determined
obstinate

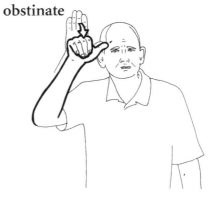

stuck
blocked
caught
trapped

student (formal)
pupil

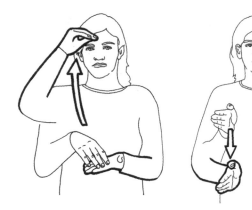

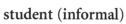

student (informal)

study

stumble
trip

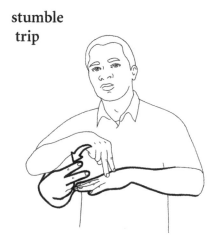

stupid
dumb
ignorant

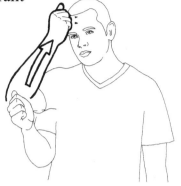

stupid
dumb
ignorant

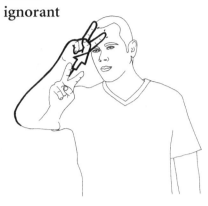

submarine

subscribe
welfare

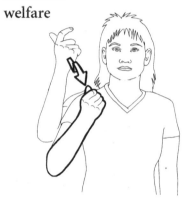

subtract
minus

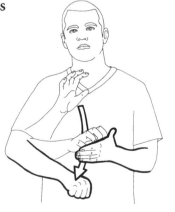

subway

Sunday

Sunday

sunrise
dawn

sunset
dusk
twilight

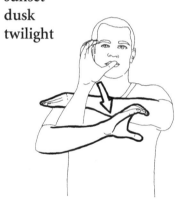

sunshine

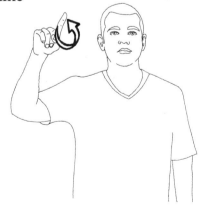

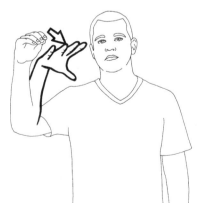

supervise

supervisor

 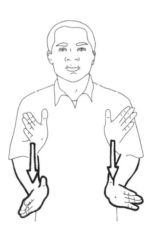

support
advocate
back
pull for
sponsor
stand behind
uphold

suppose (informal)

suppress

surface

surgeon

 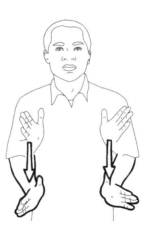

surprise
amazement
astonishment
suddenly
surprised

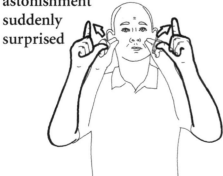

surround
surrounding

suspect (noun)

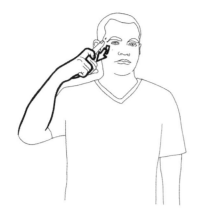

suspect (verb)

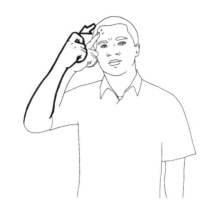

suspend
hold

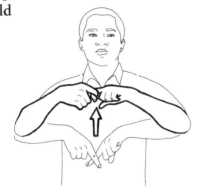

swallow

swear in court
cross heart
vow

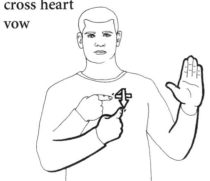

sweat
perspire

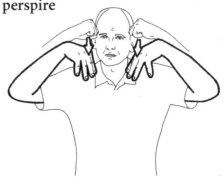

sweater
cardigan

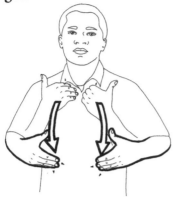

sweater
pullover

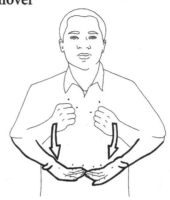

Sweden

sweep

sweetheart
honey

swell
expand

swimming
swim

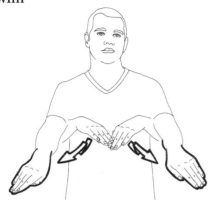

swimsuit (female)
bathing suit

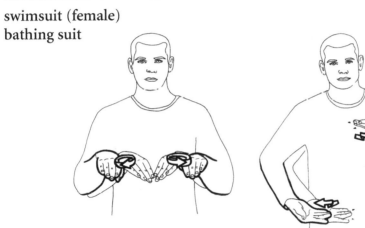

swimsuit (male)
swim trunks

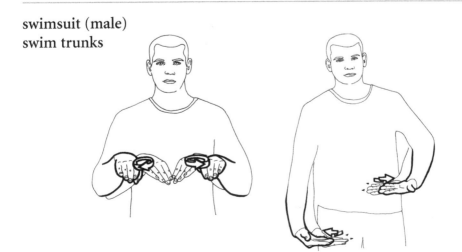

take a picture

take a pill

take turns
after
next (in line)

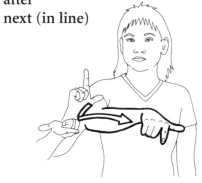

talk into a microphone

tall (people)

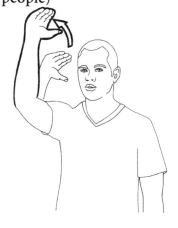

tall (objects)

tan

tank top

tap (verb)

tap dancing

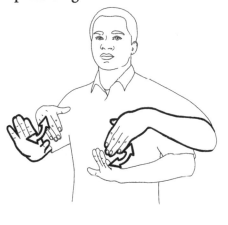

tape
scotch tape

task force (#TF)

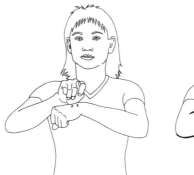

taste style	taste seasoning

tattle

tattletale

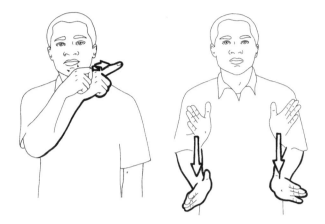

tattoo (noun)

tattoo (verb)

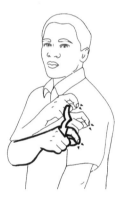

tea

teach
educate
instruct

teacher
educator
instructor
professor

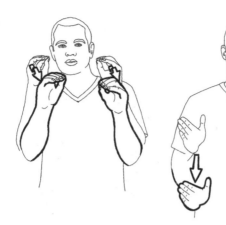

team

tears

tease
joke
kid

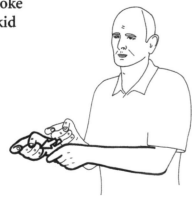

technician

technique
technical
technology

teeth

telegram

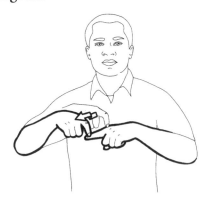

telegram

tennis

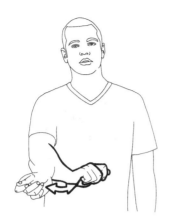

tennis net

tent

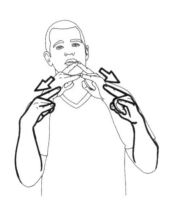

tent

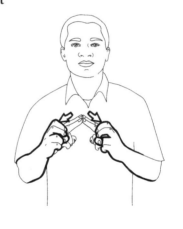

tent

terrific, excellent, exceptional, fantastic, great, marvelous, outstanding, splendid, wonderful

test
exam
examination
quiz

testament

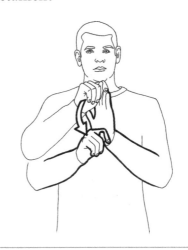

Texas

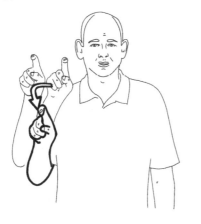

Thailand

than

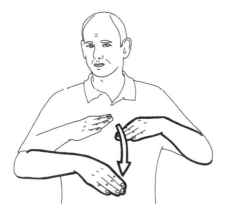

Thanksgiving

Thanksgiving

thank you
thank
thanks

that
that one

their

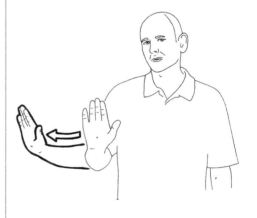

theirs

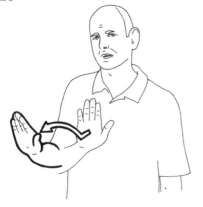

themselves

themselves

theory

there

there

therefore

thermometer

these

these

they
them

thick

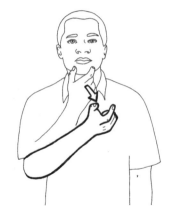

thief
burglar
robber

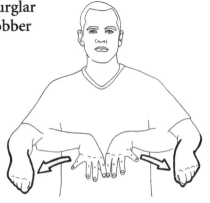

thief
burglar
robber

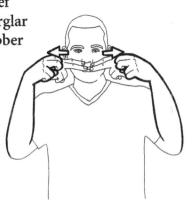

thin

thing
object

things
objects

things rolling

think
sense
thought

thinking

those two

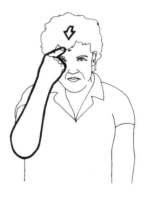

those two also
both of them
the two of them

those two also

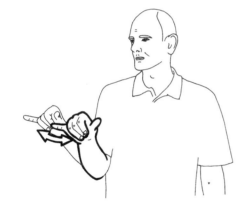

thought

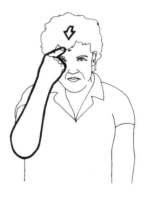

thousand

threat

three

three-fourths

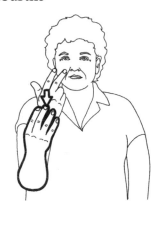

throat

through
by
via

throw

throw a baseball

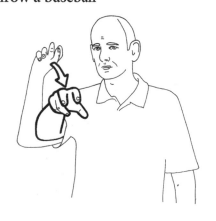

throw a basketball

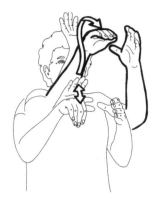

throw a softball

throw away

throw it all away

throw junk out

throw out a small object

thumb

thumbtack
push pin
tack

thunder

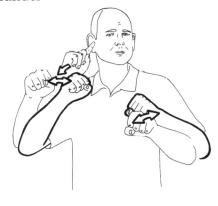

Thursday

Thursday

Tibet

tithe
one-tenth

to

toast

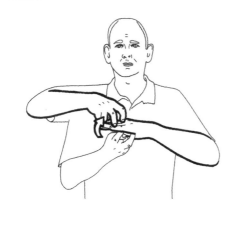

tobacco

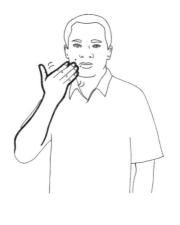

today

today
this

together

Tokyo

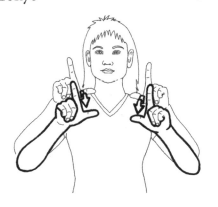

tomato

tomato

tomorrow

tongue

tonight

too long

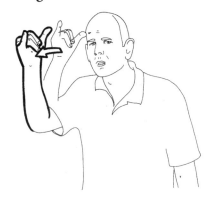

tooth

toothbrush

toothpaste

toothpaste

top
become successful
peak
top performer
(in business)

top
lid

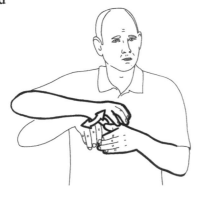

tornado

tornado

Toronto

torture (verb)
mock
put down
ridicule
torment

touch

tough
difficult
rough

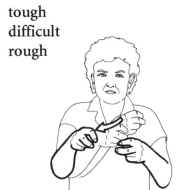

tournament
match

toward

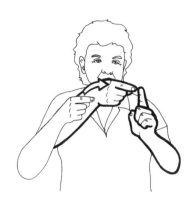

towel

town
village

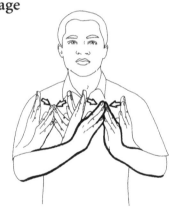

trade
instead
replace
substitute

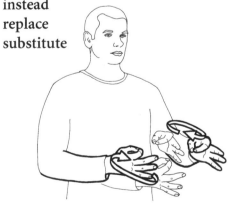

trade
instead
replace
substitute

trade places with
reverse
switch

tradition

traffic
highway

train (noun)
railroad

translate

transportation

trap

travel
tour

treasure (verb/adj.)
cherish (verb)
precious (adj.)

treasurer

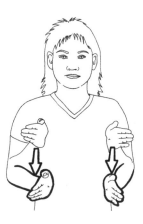

try
make an effort

T-shirt

TTY
telecommunications device
for the deaf
teletypewriter

#TTY
telecommunications device
for the deaf
teletypewriter

Tuesday

tunnel

turkey
Thanksgiving

Turkey (country)

turn
next

turn (verb)
turn around

turn around (verb)

turn down (verb)
reject
toss out

turn off

turn on

turtle
tortoise

tutor

tuxedo
bowtie
usher

twelve

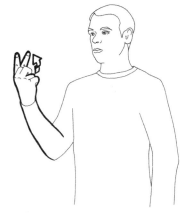

twenty

twenty-five

twenty-one

twenty-two

twins

twins

twist
sprain

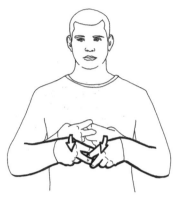

twist (squeeze an object)

twist (twist an object)

twist
wring out

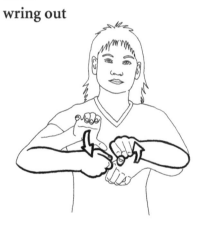

two

two more

two of us

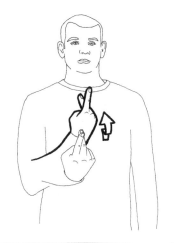

type (verb)

typewriter

ugly

umbrella

umpire
referee
whistle

university

until

up

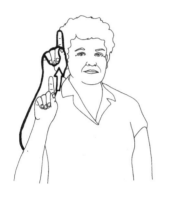

upper

upset

upside down

upstairs

urge

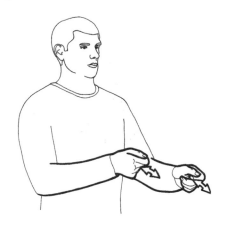

Uruguay

us
we

use
usage
useful
utilize

used to
ancient
formerly
historic
long ago

used to
habit
usual
usually

using a straw

utility meter

vacation
holiday
leave

vacuum (verb)

vacuum (verb)

vagina

vague
blurry
unclear

vain
vanity

vain
vanity

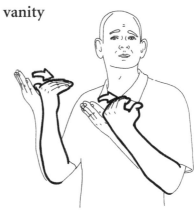

valley

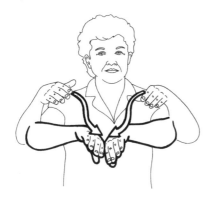

vanilla

various
diverse
varied
variety

vegetables
(Add an agent marker to this sign
for *vegetarian*.)

vein

Venezuela

verse

very

vibration

vibration

vice president (#VP)

videotape

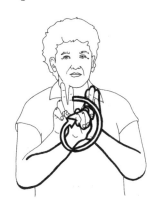

Vietnam

view

vinegar

violin

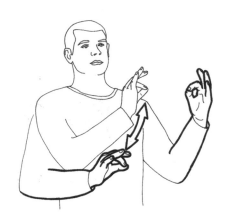

virgin

Virgin Mary

vision
dream
envision
imagine

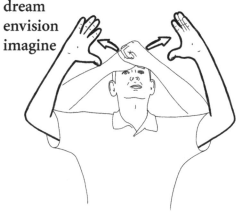

visit

visitor

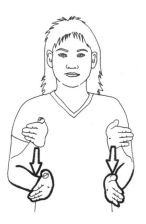

vitamin

vocabulary

vodka

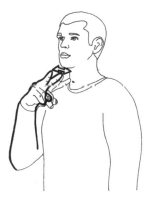

vodka

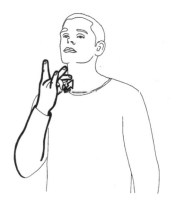

voice (noun)
volume

voice (verb)

volleyball

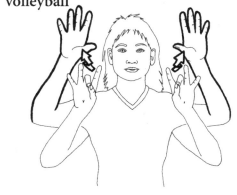

vomit
throw up

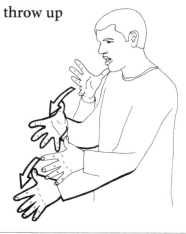

vote
elect

wag

waist

waist

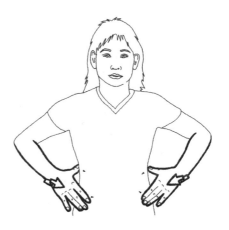

wait

wait a minute
hold on

waiter
server
waitress

waiter
server
waitress

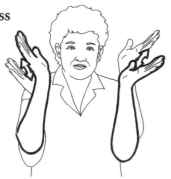

walk

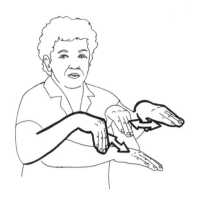

walk

walk to

wall

wallet
billfold

wall paintbrush

want

war
battle

warm

warning
caution
notice
reprimand

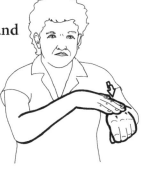

wart

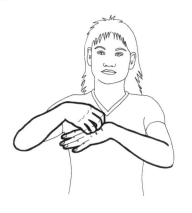

wash

wash dishes

wash face

wash face

wash hands

wash laundry

Washington, DC

Washington state

waste
squander

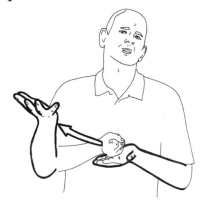

waste

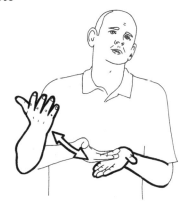

watch
wrist watch

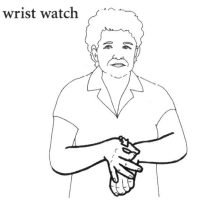

water

waterfall

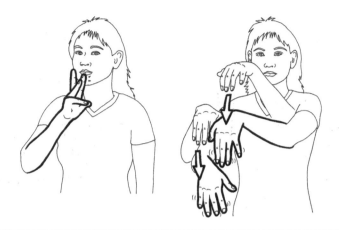

water fountain
outdoor fountain

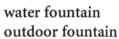
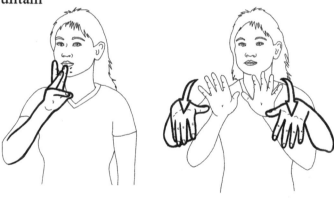

water fountain
drinking fountain
push-button fountain

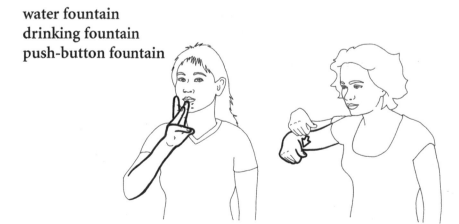

watermelon

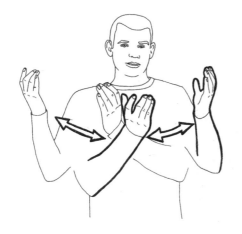

watermelon

water pump
well

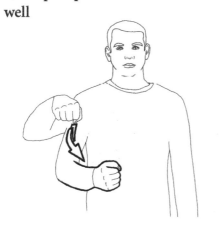

wave
get someone's attention

weak
feeble
fragile
frail
weakness

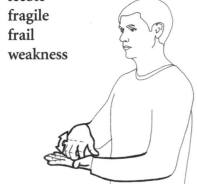

wear
use

weather
climate

weather
climate

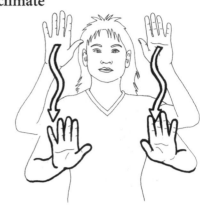

weave

wedding

Wednesday

week

weekend

weekly
every week

weigh
pound
weight

well…
so…

west
western

wet
damp
moist
moisture

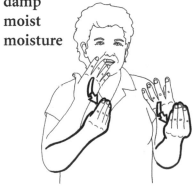

whale

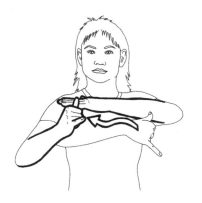

what?

what?

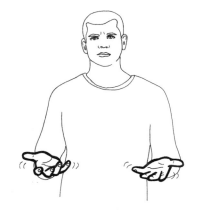

what? (#WHAT)

whatever
anyhow
anyway
doesn't matter
even though
in spite of
nevertheless
no matter
regardless

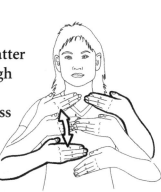

what for?
why?

what's happening?
what's going on?

what time is it?

what to do?

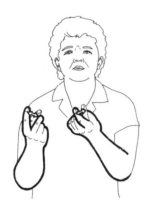

wheel

wheelbarrow

wheelchair

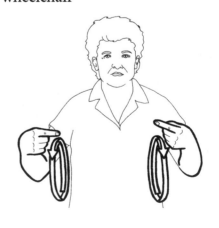

wheelchair

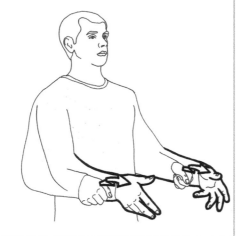

when?

where?

which?

whip (noun)

whirlpool

whiskers

whisper (in sign)

whisper (with voice)

whistle (verb)
blow a whistle

whistle (verb)

white

who?

who?

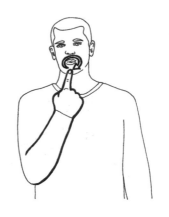

why?

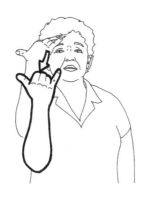

why?

wide
broad
width

wide column

wife

will
would

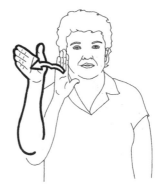

#WILL

win

wind (verb)

wind (verb)

wind (noun)
breeze
windy

window

wine

wink

wisdom

wise

wish
desire

witch

witch

with

without

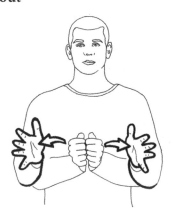

without

wolf

woman's haircut

wonder
consider
ponder

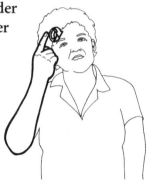

wood
lumber

woodworking
carpentry

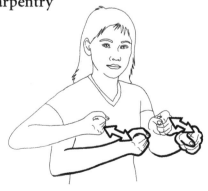

word
vocabulary

work
job
labor
task

work out
combine
fall in place
flow
merge

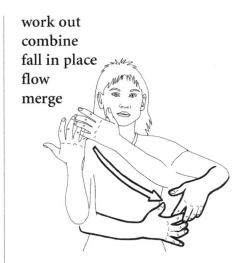

workshop

world

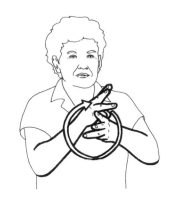

worm

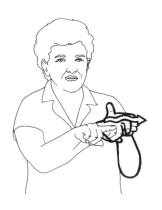

worry
anxious
fret

worse
multiply
worsen

worship
adore

worship
pray

worthless
useless

wow!

#WOW

wrap (verb)

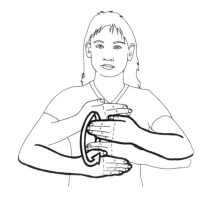

wrap (verb)
fold over

wrench

wrestle
wrestling

wrestler

wrist

wrist

write
handwrite
report

write down
note (verb)
put on
 paper
record

writer

wrong

xylophone

yawn

year

yearly
annually

yellow

yes

yes (#YES)

yesterday

yesterday

Yom Kippur

you

you (plural)
you all

young
youngster
youth
youthful

your (sing.)
yours

your (plural)
yours (plural)

yourself

yourselves

Yugoslavia

zero

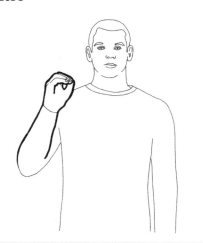

zipper

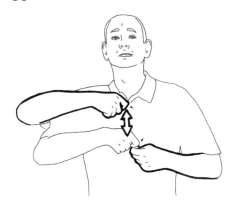

Index

An (adj.) appearing after a word indicates the adjective form of the word. A # in front of a word in capital letters indicates a lexicalized sign.